MW01420815

Train of Thought

Travel Essays from a One-Track Mind

Linda M. Au

Train of Thought

Travel Essays from a One-Track Mind

Linda M. Au

vicious circle publishing

Copyright © 2017 by Linda M. Au
Vicious Circle Publishing

All rights reserved.
No part of this book may be reproduced, stored in a retrieval system (even if I have no idea what that is) or transmitted in any form or by any means without the prior written permission of the author, except by a reviewer, who may quote brief passages in a review.
Unless it's a bad review. Then never mind.

ISBN-13: 978-1974647910
ISBN-10: 1974647919

Visit Linda online:
lindaau.com

Follow Linda on Twitter:
@LindaMAu

Stalk Linda on Facebook:
facebook.com/ AuthorLindaMAu

Ask yourself why Linda is on Instagram:
@austruck1

Cover artwork by Mike Ferrin / www.mferrin.com

vicious circle publishing

Vicious Circle Publishing
P.O. Box 133
New Brighton, PA 15066-0133
viciouscirclepublishing@gmail.com
viciouscirclepublishing.com

For Wayne,
who lets me know he still needs me
by not opening the mail or doing the laundry
while I'm out of town having adventures

Table of Contents

Acknowledgments

There are so many people who helped get this book on the right track. (Oh no, she's starting the train puns early. We're doomed.) First, I gotta thank **Catherine Lea** for giving me that initial Amtrak voucher, along with a nudge to just GO on this trip. It was a nice little bit of seed money, with an expiration date, which forced me to book my trip instead of continuing to put it off with "Someday I'll go..."

Thanks also to **Crit Club**, my inner circle of writer pals who keep me moving forward, always forward.

A hearty thanks to the **Amtrak Unlimited** forums online (with their completely non-ironic acronym of "AU"), where I learned everything I needed to know to step onto that train with a lot less fear. I still had fear, but a lot less of it.

Big hugs (always) to my parents, **Ann and John Au**, who donated to the cause in many ways, including monetarily and emotionally.

The logistics of the trip would have been a nightmare without friends such as: **Fara Linn Howell**, who (along with her daughter **Emily Reed**) got me to the station on time that first night; **Sarah Landise**, who welcomed me into her house in Kansas for two days before I continued west; **Tyler Rouse**, for giving up his bedroom for those two days while I stayed at his granna's house; **Howard and Irene Huizing**, along with the entire Los Angeles Reformed Presbyterian Church, for their gracious hospitality on the Sunday I spent in their beautiful (but oddly cold and rainy) town; **Mark McClure**, for watching my three guinea pigs (Frid, Carl, and Steve) while I was away for two weeks (although I'm not sure they really missed me all that much); **Heidi and Matt Filbert**, for taking care of the church bulletin work while I was away; the **concierge and desk clerks** at the Hyatt House hotel in Emeryville, California, for rescuing me in the middle of the night by graciously pointing me to a hotel nearby that had room for me; and **Eileen Stark**, the woman I met in the dining car who was on her way to Utah and who friended me on Facebook before the entrees came.

I also want to thank the following **Indiegogo** backers, who've been with me on this journey since the beginning—actually, since four months before I left:

Anonymous (but a huge thank-you to you anyway!)
Charlie Hull in memory of Ben Ruzicka
Jerry Hatchett
Jill Maisch
Josh and Stephanie Wilsey
Susan Lower
Jennifer Tkocs
Rachel Maize
Jeannine Dahlinger Laughman

Danielle O'Loughlin (who was thinking of being anonymous)
Hope Bowyer
Amy Mable (one of the Erma Quad)
Veryl Ann Grace
Tim Meneely
Crystal Hayduk
Fara Linn Howell
Angie Shuster (the Demon Redhead of the West)
Jackie Albertson Crouse
Nicole
Paul and Shirley Patterson
Nedra Howell
Irene Huizing
Annette Dean
Susan Campbell
Karen Moberg
The Filbert Family
Chris Bowyer
Marilyn Waltermire
Mrs. "Tali'sandGabby's Mom" Fulk
Susan Black Mensch
Lea Ryan
Tim McClain
Brooke Monroe

Last, and most importantly, I have to thank **Amtrak** for being there when I was finally ready to cross off the item that had been sitting at the top of my bucket list for decades. You did not disappoint. Special thanks to my Sleeping Car Attendants (SCAs) along the way: **José, "T,"** and **David**.

If you have a bucket list of your own, I highly recommend crossing off that top item as soon as possible. You won't regret it.

Foreword

I have a random but vivid memory of when I first moved to Pittsburgh in the early 1980s, when I was still in college. Just outside the Fort Pitt Tunnel, on the Parkway West, there is something called the Runaway Truck Sandpile. If you've never seen one of these things, let me assure you that it looks exactly the way you're probably picturing it. As you approach the tunnel heading downhill in one of two lanes, there is a third lane offshoot on the right just before the tunnel. It ends in a huge pile of gravel and sand, held in place by heavy steel drums and lots of scary pitches and angles probably thought out carefully by overpaid engineers who love to sit around and think up worst-case scenarios and then create solutions so they can get paid.

Before seeing this phenomenon, however, I had never thought about what might happen if a runaway truck careened into a tunnel, completely out of control. In fact, I had never thought about runaway trucks at all. We didn't really have tunnels in or near my hometown, and I only paid attention to tractor trailer trucks once I was sixteen and had a driver's license. By that point, they scared the crap out of me.

So, the Runaway Truck Sandpile scared me a little. Okay, a lot. No matter how huge that pile of sand and gravel was, and no matter how many heavy 55-gallon drums stood behind it to fortify it, it didn't look like enough to stop a gargantuan semi hurtling itself down the hill at breakneck speed. (Random question: How fast is "breakneck speed"?) That ridiculous pile of dirt and sandbags never fooled me for a second. If a truck went out of control there, anyone in front of it was doomed.

I don't recall ever hearing a story on the news about a runaway truck using that sandpile. But perhaps before I ever lived here, something had once happened there. Something that prompted those overthinking, worst-case-scenario engineers to come up with this solution.

And, I always assumed it was a local phenomenon.

But now I find myself sitting on a train—a much larger piece of metal machinery, one that has a phrase surrounding its own potential for losing control ("runaway train," anyone?), and we just passed a tiny little side set of tracks out here in the desert, with a tiny little pile of sand and dirt at the end of it. I mean, *tiny*. Like, the little cartoon brother of the Runaway Truck Sandpile in Pittsburgh.

I no longer find the Runaway Truck Sandpile ridiculous, because I cannot figure out what this *tiny* pile of dirt here is supposed to do for an entire train. Again, did a bunch of engineers (no pun intended this time) determine that this was enough sand and dirt to stop an oncoming train? Who knew? Apparently I should have paid more attention in physics class.

The odd thing is that I'm not frightened of traveling by train. Never have been. And now that I'm sitting on one, I'm still not afraid. Even the thought of a runaway train doesn't scare me.

Why?

At least I'm not on an airplane.

Introduction

I try to stop myself from typing "Amtrak sleeper" in the Google Images search box. But it's no use. I'm off on another daydream about what it will be like when I first step out of that cab a few months from now, armed with nothing more than a backpack and a messenger bag, each full of things I've deemed essential for survival for the next two weeks.

What will it be like to sit in the Amtrak station here in Pittsburgh in that last hour before I am no longer a train-virgin? How many other people will be there waiting with me? Will some be so used to this routine that they'll be nodding off or looking bored? How will I not stick out like the newbie I am?

And what will it finally be like when I climb onto that first train, headed for Chicago overnight and then points west? I've chosen a simple coach seat for those first nine hours, which will come between midnight and nine a.m. I saved my money for the roomette upgrades later in the trip. I know I'll be too keyed up that first night and won't sleep anyway. Might as well sit in my roomy, comfortable coach seat (I finally found a benefit of being 5'1"), with my little laptop open, typing my eager thoughts about the train—the sights, the sounds, the smells (but Lord, don't let there be too many smells!).

Today, though, more than three months before my trip, I open a search engine and type in the word "Amtrak," and thousands of images pop up. Many I've seen before, since I do this dumb sort of daydreaming at least once a week. Now that I've purchased the tickets and the trip is set, I suspect I'll daydream my way through many lulls in my daily schedule. And I admit, sometimes I fall asleep trying to imagine what it will be like once I am cocooned in a tiny roomette, where I will wake up hundreds of miles from where I fell asleep.

Oh sure, I've done similar things on a plane. And on a cruise ship. But soon, I will do this on my very first train trip. The trip of a lifetime. My lifetime, at least. What adventures await me? What misadventures? I'm ready for all of them.

Bring it on, Amtrak. I'm ready to see America.

How It Began:
The Indiegogo Campaign

My bucket list is fairly modest. No climbing Mount Kilimanjaro or running with the bulls. No exotic locales or personal challenges that are beyond my abilities. The top of my bucket list has always been taking a cross-country train trip. Alone. An adventure just for me, not shared with anyone else. (Well, except you guys.) Not even going anywhere in particular. Just hopping on a train, heading across the country from east to west and back again.

Keep reading. It gets better.

At one point last year I realized that making this trip happen was entirely up to me. Nobody from Amtrak was going to knock on my door like Publishers Clearing House, standing on my porch with a handful of balloons and a big cardboard train ticket. I was going to have to do this on my own.

So, I did what any normal person would do, taking the first steps to plan a trip of this magnitude:

I hired a cartoonist.

I knew I'd be able to get a whole book's worth of stories out of this trip. And I'd worked with cartoonist Mike Ferrin on several other projects before this. He did the amazing artwork for the covers of several of my books ([shameless plug] *Head in the Sand... and other unpopular positions; Fork in the Road... and other pointless discussions; The Scarlet Letter Opener*; the upcoming *The Tell-Tale Heart Attack,* among others). I asked if he was ready for another obnoxious challenge from me. He was totally on board with it. (Get it? Train puns. Get used to them.)

As usual, he hit the ball outta the park on the cover art. We tweaked a few things along the way and ended up with the artwork you see here.

When I attended the Erma Bombeck Writers' Workshop in March 2016, I knew I'd need a *complete* cover (not just the artwork) to add to a brochure I wanted to bring along for self-promotion. Cue cover designer Rachel Cole from Littera Designs. I've known Rachel for more than a decade, having shared membership with her in Crit Club—a small, private online writers group—for many years. She's not only a fellow writer; she's also an amazing cover designer. Because I also proofread and typeset book interiors, we sometimes exchange services. I sent over the artwork and told her what text needed to go on the front cover ASAP so I could print up the brochures for the conference.

In less than a half hour, she shot back what she said was a preliminary mock-up. She probably did it while she was doing twelve other things. She's just that amazing, and she's a font nerd like I am. I liked her hastily prepared mock-up so much that you're essentially seeing it here on the front cover of this book. Her intuitive sense of good font choices continues to amaze me. All I had to do was fiddle with a back cover and I was set.

Once I had sunk time and money into getting a cover, I had to *take the trip and write the book*. Sure, it was a little backwards to start with a cartoonist before I'd ever done research into the possibilities of an actual trip. But, what could go wrong now? I had a purpose. I had a book cover. I was almost there. All I had to do was *take the trip and write the book.*

Then I researched the costs. Then I hyperventilated into a paper bag trying to recover from researching the costs. It turns out that train travel—long-distance train travel, at least—can get rather pricey if you don't want to sit in the same seat day and night for six or seven thousand miles. I had assumed that the cost of train travel would fall somewhere between a bus ticket and a plane ticket. Turns out it falls between the cost of a plane ticket and a space shuttle ticket. I was devastated to learn that this trip would cost me several thousand dollars, even though I wasn't actually going anywhere.

Undeterred, I rearranged some of my personal finances, but still the numbers weren't where I wanted them. Travel purely for its own sake now seemed frivolous. If only I could shave off a few of the expenses, I could manage this in good conscience.

Then it hit me: crowdfunding. There's an entire website dedicated to crowdfunding for creative projects. Naturally I'd be writing about my experiences as I traveled. The site has an entire section for writers crowdfunding book projects. Cue glorious, uplifting, classical music.

And that's how my campaign on Indiegogo was born.

I decided on a modest goal: not funding the entire trip, but only slightly less than half of it. My parents had taught me that you don't truly appreciate something if you don't have to work for it. Of course, I'm in my fifties and still think that's bullshit, because I get pretty excited when somebody gives me something for free. But hey, it made me look slightly more noble if I asked for a thousand dollars from the outside world, instead of two or three thousand.

I wrote up the campaign and held my breath...

Here's the Basic Campaign as it appeared online. Updates I wrote to the backers appear chronologically throughout the book.

Put humor writer Linda Au on a train for the first time. Let her travel across the country with little more than a backpack and a laptop. Let her attention to detail kick in along the way. Let her come home two weeks later with the makings of a travelogue filled with a little awe, a little wonder, and a lot of weirdness. In the end, you'll have *Train of Thought: Travel Essays from a One-Track Mind.*

Welcome to my Train of Thought!

Howdy! I'm humor writer and novelist Linda M. Au. You probably haven't heard of me yet. *Yet.* If you have heard of me, then you're probably related to me or sat next to me in math class in the 1970s. But let's move right along...

A cross-country train trip has always been at the top of my bucket list. And, let's face it, I ain't gettin' any younger.

So, what happens when a humor writer decides to finally live her dream? (Not the one where I marry Gene Wilder and we live on a cruise ship. THIS dream! The bucket list!)

Naturally, she gets on that train and brings along her laptop and writes about the experience. In glorious, humorous detail.

This is how the book *Train of Thought: Travel Essays from a One-Track Mind* will be born.

And YOU can be part of it!

What I Need & What You Get

The trip itself will occur in early May 2017.

Here are all the gory details:

- **Sitting** on a train, **sleeping** in a tiny cubicle, **staring** out a window, and **eating** dining car food all cost money. I'm hoping to fund half the trip through this campaign.
- The end result will be a **book**. A hilarious, marvelous, clever book.
- A few months after the trip, contributors at various levels will receive **copies of the completed book**: the Kindle edition, the paperback edition, etc. Higher contributions will include copies of my other books as well (to be chosen by the contributor).
- All contributors will also receive exclusive **updates during the trip** itself. I'll post interesting tidbits and snippets en route at Wi-Fi hotspots along the way.

All contributions will go toward the cost of the **train ticket**, which will be about twice what I hope to raise here.

The rest of the costs of the trip will come from me. After all, I'm the one who gets to sleep in a tiny cubicle, to meet people I may not like, and to get stuck on a loud, moving vehicle for two weeks straight with fewer clothes and toiletries than I am comfortable with...

Risks & Challenges

There is the risk that the trip will be a completely smooth, wonderful, beautiful experience and that absolutely nothing funny will happen for the entire two weeks.

But, c'mon. Anybody who knows me knows that's **not** going to happen. The challenge is going to be quite the opposite... shutting myself up once I start yammering on about all the outrageous, silly, crazy stuff I'll experience as I cross the country by myself, all alone for two solid weeks on a tra—*oh geez, what was I thinking?*

Oh, sorry. Did I just type that out loud? Carry on. Nothing to see here.

Other Ways You Can Help

If you can't contribute right now, that's totally fine. I still need to get the word out about the trip, about the book, about any of my books. Use the Indiegogo share tools here to pass the word along to others who might be interested. You know: other writers, fellow readers, train enthusiasts, people with a sense of humor, introverts... and, of course, introverted train enthusiast writers with a sense of humor. Both of them.

Thanks!

The Campaign Months:
Indiegogo Backer Updates Before the Trip

January 1, 2017

Happy New Year, Everyone!

It's 2017, the Year of the Train Trip! (That's kind of like the Year of the Rat in China, right? Gosh, I hope that rat thing isn't literal.)

Four short months from now I'll be scurrying and scampering around the house (sorry for that awkward image—you can't unsee that in your mind), doing some last-minute packing and prep.

Here in Pittsburgh, the train will leave around midnight, as it always does. (Who makes these schedules? Midnight? Seriously?) Will I sleep that first night on my way to Chicago? No way. I predict I'll be sitting bolt upright in my coach seat, clutching my backpack, staring out the window into the darkness, trying not to hyperventilate. And trying not to think of *Strangers on a Train* or *Murder on the Orient Express*.

And that just can't be a good way to start off a trip of this magnitude. (Note to self: Add "smelling salts" to packing list.)

Stay tuned!

January 10, 2017

Already I'm Confused ...

I bought a money belt for this trip. I'm not sure if I already feel safer, or if I'm going to end up in a seedy hostel in California, bleeding in a bathtub with my pancreas harvested for money. (Joke's on them, though. I'm diabetic. You couldn't give my pancreas away on Craigslist, even if you tacked on a free Hatchimal.)

The money belt itself is fine, but it came with a little flyer labeled "Useful Travel Safety Tips." I'm eager to read anything that even tangentially relates to this trip, so I sat down to read through their list of fifty helpful (and not-so-helpful) tips. Here's a glimpse for the voyeuristic among you:

"If possible, take a self-defense class."

Great. This hadn't even occurred to me. Do fistfights routinely break out on Amtrak trains? There'll be a fight over the good seats in the observation car somewhere around Colorado, won't there?

"Bring a portable door or window alarm."

The first time I read that, I saw "Bring a portable door" and panicked that the trains might not have doors. Still, even with the rest of the sentence factored in, I find this suggestion a little disturbing.

"Be on the lookout for anybody who is offering to help you with your bags at a train or bus station."

Because it would be horrible if a Red Cap actually *helped* me lug that suitcase up to my roomette! The horrors!

These next four are back to back on the flyer:

"Trust your instincts and use your intuition and gut feeling when dealing with strangers."
"Make a local friend."
"Try to dress like a local."
"In some places, it helps wearing a fake wedding ring."

I don't even know where to start with these four. All I know is that, by the time I finished reading #3, I had so many questions that I was weeping uncontrollably.

- What if my gut instincts tell me *not* to make a local friend?
- To dress like a local in Los Angeles, do I have to wear an Ed Hardy shirt and Birkenstocks and grow a hipster beard?
- Why can't I just wear my real wedding ring? After all, it looks fake in the right lighting...

"If you get lost, do not look at your phone or a map in the middle of the street."

... because you'll get hit by a car. Duh.

There are forty-two more of these gems in this flyer. After reading them all, I may not be able to work up the courage to get to the station, let alone get on the train.

Onward and upward...

January 16, 2017

Fly the Friendly Skies

O*verheard in the grocery store... Wait, no, overheard in* my mind *(sorry, I get the two confused). A conversation with myself...*

"Linda, why on earth would you take a train trip across the country for two weeks, when you could fly across and back in a single day?"

"Well, Alt-Linda, I hate flying."

"So do birds, Linda, but you don't see them complaining."

"Birds don't hate flying."

"Well, you get my point, though."

"No, not really."

"You actually hate flying?"

"No, I'm just faking all those heart palpitations and that vomiting whenever a plane trip gets closer. Like, a year in advance."

"But why take a train? For two weeks? To essentially do nothing but take the train?"

"Think of the adventure, Alt-Linda! The romantic lure of the rails! The glorious susurrus of the train as it glides across landscapes far and wide!"

"Susurrus? You just made that up."

"No, it's a real word. Honest. Look it up."

"I'd have to know how to spell it to look it up."

"Well, it's right here on the screen."

"Not yet it's not. You're still transcribing this conversation. And it's not even a real conversation. It's just you talking to yourself. Again."

"Don't be a smart-ass. It's going to be an adventure, Alt-Linda. I can't wait!"

"You're lucky this conversation is all in your head. I bet you can't pronounce *susurrus*."

"Shut up. Nobody's talking to you."

"Except you."

"I'm you. Well, you know what I mean."

"Rarely, but let's move on. So, let me get this straight. You're going to pay these Amtrak people a lot of money—"

"I already did. They charged my credit card, like, a nanosecond after I clicked 'Submit.'"

"Okay, so, you already paid these Amtrak people a lot of money to sit in a big metal box on wheels that's going to go careening across the country at nowhere-near-breakneck speed... for two weeks."

"Well, yes, but..."

"And at periodic intervals you're going to go to a different metal box on wheels—attached to the first box on wheels and a bunch of other boxes on wheels—to get expensive food."

"It's included in the price, though."

"Which was expensive."

"You're completely missing the point."

"And at other periodic intervals you're going to lie down and sleep in your original metal box—in a teeny, smaller box inside the bigger metal box, a box so small that they'll give you a crowbar to get in and out of bed."

"It's included in the price, though."

"Which was expen—"

"Okay, okay. What's your point?"

"We haven't even made it to Chicago yet in this scenario. Do I really need a point?"

"But it's going to be—"

"If you use the word 'adventure' one more time I'm going to smack you."

"That'd be quite a trick."

"Back to your flawed thinking: If you get bored in the teeny tiny metal box or aren't hungry enough to go to the metal food box—"

"They have tablecloths in the dining car."

"Oh, well, THAT changes everything."

"I sense sarcasm."

"Moi?"

"I still don't see your point."

"My point, Linda, is that your definition of 'adventure' is rather low, don't you think?"

"Potato, potahto."

"You're always bringing up food."

"Only when I think about flying."

"That's a gross, disgusting play on words."

"You're the one who brought up bringing up food."

"Back to my original point! Where's your sense of

adventure if all you're doing is sitting in big metal boxes, eating food, sleeping, writing, and showering in tiny cubicles with flexible hoses recently used by complete strangers?"

"I'm bringing my Kindle along."

"That's it. I'm outta here. Taxi!"

"Don't call for a taxi. Take the train."

"You're out of your mind."

"No, you're out of my mind."

"Oh, shut up!"

January 30, 2017

Safety Precautions

Don't get over-excited, but I bought a new wallet for the train trip. What's wrong with my current wallet? Nothing, really. Except this new one not only holds my credit cards, cash, and travel documents, but also will do my laundry and help me memorize the entire New Testament. At least, that's what I'm guessing based on the little insert that came with it. I'm reproducing the text exactly as it appears—typos, bad punctuation, and odd capitalization included.

I'm not doing this to mock whatever bad online translation program they probably utilized to go from Chinese to English. I'm merely asking myself this: does it seem as if they assume English-speaking folks need to have things repeated many times, with slightly different wording, in order to remember them?

I offer you the following, without commentary, if only because some things need no explanation:

• *This High Density linen/cotton blended fabric All-in-One Passport Holder fits your iphone, Holding Passport, Boarding Card, Credit Cards, Tickets. Coins, Keys, money, other documents, etc.*

• *The Passport Wallet is simple, compact, lightweight, zippered and multifunctional. Portable and Compact case, is easily held in Handbag passport holder. men's and women's travel gear case. An ideal travel accessory holder, a nice cover for your passport.*

• *Best travel documents holder with smooth Closing Zipper, secure wallet that protects your travel accessories. A zip around travel wallet for your convenience.*

• *Durable travel wallet with multiple pockets, perfect for all your needed documents.*

• *A slim small wallet for holding and making easy to access your documents while traveling. Fits your hand, your bag, and your jacket pocket.*

Doesn't this make you want to go out and buy twelve of these wallets? Or invest in company stock? Or stab someone?

February 11, 2017

Campaign Success!

Thanks to all of you marvelous backers for a successful, fun campaign! I couldn't have done it without you!

Well, technically, I could have, but it would have been a pointless waste of time to write up an entire campaign only to donate a thousand bucks to myself and then watch Indiegogo take a cut. I've done stupider things, but not lately.

Anyway, where was I? Oh yeah, I was thanking you lovable, wacky knuckleheads...

Thanks!

Thanks to you, now the credit card company will stop throwing panicky fits over that huge charge I made to Amtrak a few weeks ago.

I've already made quite a few notes for the book, and I haven't even left yet. But of course, a strangely introspective trip like this is going to start in my head months ahead of time. That's the beauty of our overthinking, introvert brains: we never stop asking, "What if?" We are the kings and queens of the Worst-Case Scenario.

The official trip starts in **early May**, around midnight here in Pittsburgh. Due to my husband's work schedule at that time, he can't drive me to the station. So I'll start off with a cab ride to the train station downtown. And I'm already obsessing over whether the cab will show up on time. (Just **ONE** time I called a cab in the 1990s and it was late, and I'll never let myself forget it.)

Once I acclimated to the idea of a cab, though, I realized I might as well start the trip off with an introvert's worst nightmare: sitting alone late at night in a small vehicle with a stranger who will drop me off in a desolate part of the downtown area. Yay!

And of course it will be smooth sailing from there. Right? Because... what could go wrong?*

**rhetorical question, not meant for actual answers*

March 1, 2017

The Train Tracks Less Traveled

Okay, a few of you are wondering exactly where I'm going when I get on that midnight train to Georgia—I mean, *Chicago*. (Free earworm with every donation!) After much mumbling and scribbling, I came up with a graphic showing my train routes (and showing why I am not an artist).

The black line shows my westward journey from Pittsburgh to Seattle (through Los Angeles). Then I start back (again through Los Angeles) on the gray route.** I'll be getting off the train to stay locally several times along the way, but will otherwise be on a train the rest of those two weeks.

I'm finalizing the packing list (doesn't everyone take two months to make a packing list?) and getting the rest of my affairs in order. You know, important stuff like making sure the squirrel and shark puppets will both fit in the backpack, getting the guinea pigs' nails trimmed at the vet's, and making out a proper last will and testament. (I'm an optimist who enjoys running worst-case scenarios.)

It's going to be quite an adventure! Or else!

***Four days before I left, Amtrak canceled the Seattle portion of my trip due to a service disruption. Apparently these things happen. And apparently they piss me off.*

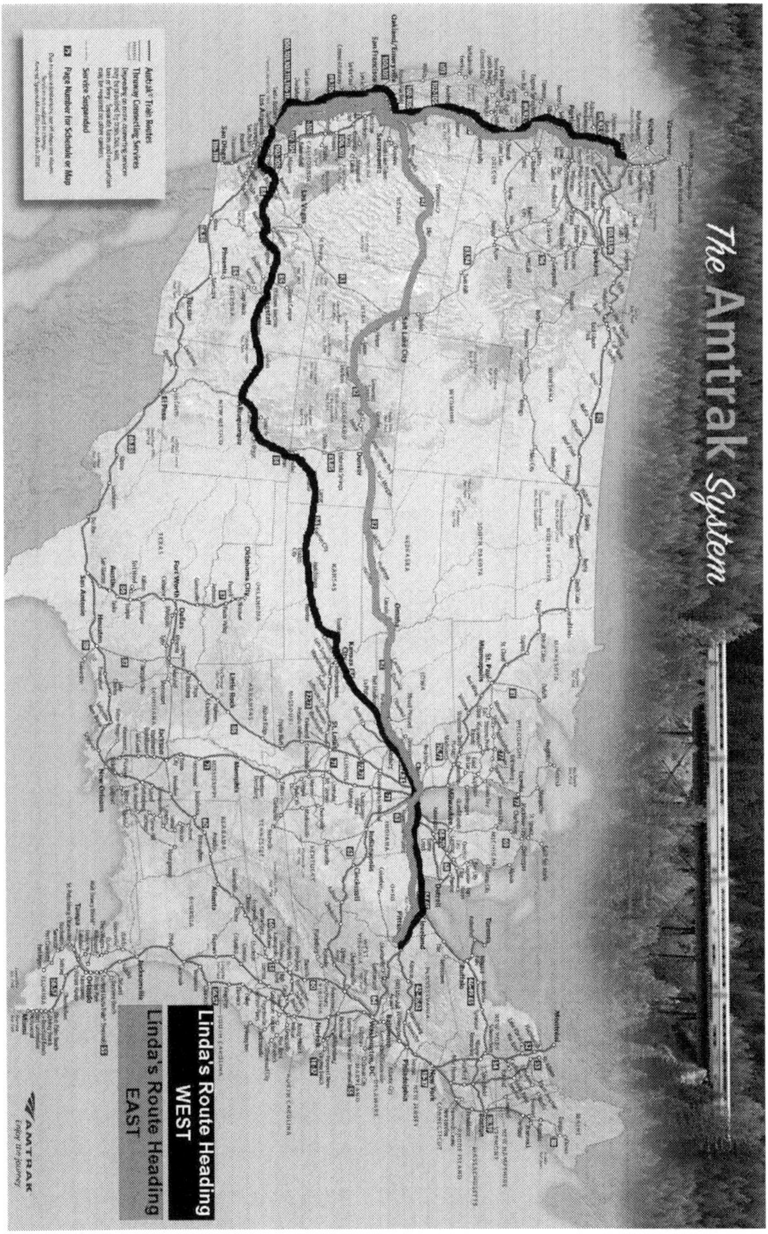
The Amtrak System
Linda's Route Heading WEST
Linda's Route Heading EAST
AMTRAK

April 17, 2017

Tick-Tock, Tick-Tock…

The clock is ticking! Either that, or there's a bomb in my office. (I think I've been watching too many back episodes of *The Blacklist*.)

In just about two weeks I'll be scurrying around the house, packing that ***one*** backpack and that ***one*** messenger bag for my two-week train adventure. Right now, as I look at the items I need to pack, which are collecting on the work table in my office, I think the biggest adventure will be fitting everything into those two bags.

My packing list is a two-page Word document (I always make packing lists in Word, don't you?), and I continue to tweak it—adding things here, deleting things there (though not deleting nearly enough things there). The document also includes a to-do list of stuff that needs to be done before I can leave Pittsburgh. That's always the worst part of packing for a trip.

Sometime in the final days before I leave, I'll print the whole document out and carry it around like a talisman (or a love letter from "Weird Al" Yankovic).

I tend to write down everything imaginable on these lists so that I don't forget something. In the final frenetic hours before I leave, I'll be crossing things off the list that I've decided *not* to do, *not* to pack. The to-do list, especially, always includes things that are little more than wishful thinking (like, spring cleaning the entire house and scrubbing the base boards before I leave). Those are the sorts of things that go first. *Nope, I don't need to solve pi to a thousand places before I leave. And honestly, why did I put "learn tai chi" on the list? And how did "download edible recipes for kale" get on there?*

The packing list is more of a challenge. I've already started paring that down, but some of the things on it just have to stay there. I mean, I'm *not* leaving Boris the squirrel home! He's my mascot, and he was crocheted into being by a friend specifically for this trip.

Let's hope I don't go overboard crossing things off this list, or I might not pack any underwear and end up hand-washing the pair I'm wearing in a bathroom sink and hanging it in the roomette to dry.

And last I heard, there just isn't enough room in a roomette for that.

And So It Begins . . .

Day One

May 1, 2017

I woke up today thinking, "Today is the day." Then I thought, "I'm hungry." Then I thought, "I should really pee first before I do anything else."

After that, things kinda went downhill. Yesterday I took the three guinea pigs—Frid, Carl, and Steve—to board with my friend Mark while I'm away, and today I keep forgetting they're not here in their cage in my office. So I'm talking to the empty cage as I finish my packing, wondering why I don't hear a familiar "wheek!" in reply. Now I'm worried that I'll keep doing this, talking to myself once I'm at the station, or, worse, on the train. I could end up in a strait-jacket before I even get to Chicago. Great.

I think I'm almost ready to leave. I've washed all the laundry and stocked the fridge and pantry with Wayne's favorite snacks. I've tidied up the house a bit (*a bit*) and taken the trash to the curb. I'm looking around the house this morning, and everything seems to be in place. The backpack and messenger bag are packed, too, so I'm as ready as I'm going to be for my big adventure.

Even though the train doesn't leave Pittsburgh till midnight tonight, I won't see Wayne till after I get home in nearly two weeks. He left for work right after I fed him breakfast, and my parents are taking me to where my friend Fara works this afternoon so she can taxi me to the train station later on tonight. I've tried explaining the logistics of this to Wayne, who heard only, "I won't be home to make dinner." This probably explains the abject sadness in his eyes... but then his mood brightens when he realizes this means he can eat fast food and Chinese buffets till I'm back. Glad to see he's going to miss me.

By the time Wayne gets home tonight, he will have forgotten everything I told him this morning, including that I am leaving town, especially since my car will still be in the driveway. Sometime around Day Eight he'll think to himself, "Where's Linda?" Probably right around the same time he runs out of clean underwear or Klondike bars. In our world, those two things are of equal importance.

I spend the rest of the afternoon putzing on the computer, making sure I've answered every email, checked every bank account, paid every bill, jotted down the balances on all the credit cards, and updated Facebook with pre-trip posts that excite nobody but me. Let's face it: if I don't leave soon, I'm going to bore nearly a thousand Facebook friends to death with my obnoxious, never-ending posts about this trip. I can only hope that the posts get more interesting once I'm actually on a train and outside of Pittsburgh. Nobody needs any more posts about the type of shampoo I'm packing.

My parents show up right on time and we load my gear into their car and head for Ambridge to meet Fara before she leaves for work. Until recently I had assumed I'd be taking a taxi to the train station tonight. Wayne couldn't drop me off because of his early work schedule. And my parents seem to go to bed right after dinner—and everyone knows retired people eat dinner around three p.m. It's required by law. I think they make old people sign some sort of waiver about not being seen after the sun goes down in order to get their Social Security.

So, Mom and Dad couldn't take me downtown late at night, either. I'm not sure they could *find* downtown Pittsburgh even in broad daylight. You know, they've only lived here for *thirteen years,* and despite having come back east after a decade of living in burgeoning Las Vegas, they fear driving anywhere near downtown Pittsburgh the way some people fear the plague or Ebola or Hillary Clinton. I can't say I blame them, really. The streets and bridges around the downtown area are confusing. We don't have a beltway. We don't have square city blocks with right angles. We have oddly placed one-way streets in the middle of the business district. There are more yellow bridges than you can count. And all the bridges have about five lanes of traffic across them, with three or four lanes feeding onto the bridges and then another three or four separate lanes feeding off the other side. And everybody feeding in from the left lanes always needs to get over to the right lanes in that fifty yards across the bridge. It's a nightmare.

I'm getting hives just typing about it.

This is why I cannot ask my parents to take me to the train station at ten p.m. on a school night. (The school night part doesn't have anything to do with it. I just threw that in there in honor of all the times I wasn't allowed to do anything as a kid because it was a school night.) Besides, my parents haven't driven after dark since sometime in the Clinton Administration. You know, the other Clinton. The one with the Y chromosome. No, *BILL*.

Anyway, for months I'd been weighing the pros and cons of taking a taxi or an Uber to get to the train station, which is about thirty or forty miles from my house. Estimates were running about $100 for that forty-five-minute cab ride. I wasn't too happy about that. I'd practically max out a credit card just getting to the station before even leaving. Not cool.

Then Fara suggested that, if I could get to her place of employment by the time she left for the day, I could hang out at her house for a while and she'd get me to the train station that night. After all, she lives only a hop, skip, and a jump from downtown. It was settled. I had my ride. I'd worry about how to get back home after the trip later. Like, twelve days from now.

Fara, her daughter Emily, and I grab dinner at a nearby Eat'n Park restaurant and talk about a lot of girly nothings, which I always find great fun. I never get to talk girly nothings with Wayne at dinner, for some reason. Heck, to be honest, Wayne almost never talks at all at dinner. For one thing, there's food in front of him. For another thing, the man doesn't talk unless the house is on fire or a new season of *Survivor* is starting that night. For a third thing, there's still food in front of him. So, giggling with Fara and Emily is a perfect way to spend some of my final hours before the trip tonight.

After dinner we still have time to kill, so Fara takes us to Target to pick up a few things. I'm focused on finding single-load laundry detergent pods. I'll be doing laundry when I hit California, so that I can make the return trip east without having to apologize to everyone else on the train for the body odor. The pods I have at home are too big to fit into the cute little plastic container I bought, so I'm hoping to find travel-size pods or something similar. No dice. This store doesn't have much of a travel-size section. I'll have to deal with the laundry detergent question when I'm in my hotel in Los Angeles.

Instead, I buy more granola bars, just in case.

9:00 p.m.

Fara and Emily have just dropped me off at the Amtrak station in the heart of downtown Pittsburgh. Frankly, the exterior of this station isn't the most welcoming sight—not since they started using the beautiful Penn Station upstairs as a wedding and event venue, having set up a modest but functional station waiting room downstairs near some cement walls with peeling paint and about five dark, secluded parking spots. *Amtrak welcomes you to Pittsburgh.* Sort of. Just don't loiter around down here, okay?

But I'm leaving Pittsburgh, not arriving, and I'm too keyed up to notice the peeling paint tonight. I have a momentary seize-up of my heart as Fara drives away because now I'm truly alone among strangers for most of the next twelve days. And although I, as an introvert, typically love to wallow in the word "alone," I like to do that from the comfort and safety of my own home. Not on a huge public mode of transportation where I'll be sharing meals and bathrooms and shower stalls and...

Wait! Fara, come back!

Alas, she is gone, and I'm forced to head into the Amtrak waiting room alone. I step inside, with my backpack hoisted over my right shoulder and my messenger bag clutched in my left hand. It's a little too warm in here, but not suffocating. I survey the scene and grab the closest seats that aren't surrounded by other people. Now I'm off in a corner near the door where I just came in, one arm slung protectively across my backpack and messenger bag in the adjoining seat as I scribble notes in a little notebook I bought just for the trip. There are about a dozen Amish people here among those of us awaiting the train, some of them speaking their own hybrid brand of German. I know it's a modified form of the language because I took German for five years in junior high and high school (and a semester in college), and this sounds only marginally like that.

Not that I remember all that much from all those classes all those years ago. Stuff like "ach du lieber!" stays with me, and several verb forms I won't repeat here, and the fact that German nouns are about twenty-seven consonants too long and often make you spit on people. What I'm hearing from across the waiting room isn't quite like that. Plus, I'm hearing English words tossed in every so often, just to throw me off. (I swear I'm not paranoid. I *know* all these Amish people are judging me for my complete lack of fashion sense. I just know it. Snobs.)

There's also a middle-aged hipster in a bank of seats to my left. I'm unsure what to think about this man. He looks about my age or a little older, and he's got skinny jeans, those trendy hiking sandals with adjustable straps everywhere, a huge duffel-backpack thing that I immediately covet, and what I think might be an Ed Hardy shirt. I'm not entirely certain, though, because I'm completely unhip and not sure

I've ever seen an actual Ed Hardy shirt in the wild. I do own an ancient pair of Birkenstocks. That's as close as I get to being hipster. I gave up on the beard idea years ago.

Now a few young Amish men have also come into the waiting room and gravitated to the seats just in front of the wall-mounted flat-screen television. I glance around the waiting room, which has begun to fill up a little more, and see that the Amish are the only ones not glued to their smartphones. For obvious reasons. Well, them and the old hipster guy. He's busy fiddling with his Moleskine notebook and his fountain pen. Everyone else—including a man with a blind person's white cane with the red tip—is using their smartphones. I'm not sure what to think about the guy with the cane, so I whip out my phone, find a Wi-Fi hotspot (since I have no data on my cheapie phone), and post an update on Facebook. If you can't beat 'em, join 'em.

11:30 p.m.

An announcement over the loudspeaker informs us that the train scheduled for 11:59 p.m. will be arriving around 12:20 a.m. instead. No one reacts. A few people yawn. Similar news in an airport would have sent people screaming and yelling for a ticket counter. Not here. Apparently anything within an hour of the scheduled arrival or departure time is considered no big deal. I immediately sense that this mode of transportation is entirely different from airline travel. Which is fine with me because I hate flying. And screaming and yelling.

Other people have meandered in, including a young millennial couple (possibly hipster—I haven't decided yet) dressed mostly in black. He's wearing a fedora. She's wearing, well, black. The Amish are more colorfully dressed than these two. Definitely hipster.

Speaking of the Amish (again), a handful of Amish youth head for the vending machines for some coffee and stand there staring at the contraption for a while. I wonder if perhaps they've never used one before. Eventually they figure it out and head back to their seats in front of the television with their coffee cups.

All Aboard!

It's no surprise that we are on the lower level of the station and would normally take an escalator up to the platform, carrying all our luggage. For a moment I feel smug that I have managed to pack everything in a single backpack and one messenger bag. For a *brief* moment. Because it's also no surprise that tonight the escalator isn't working and we have to lug everything up about a hundred steps. By the time I'm at the top there's already a crowd of people and I'm gasping for air because this messenger bag weighs a ton. Laptop, tablet, Kindle, two weeks of toiletries and medications, paperwork, notebook, pens, half a million granola bars...

I fleetingly wish I'd used something with wheels, but lugging that up all those stairs wouldn't have been any easier. Why don't they make hover-bags or drone bags or balloon bags or something? I'm going to jot this down for a Kickstarter project once I'm back home. I'd totally buy one.

After taking a few deep breaths, I look around to see a sea of people. When did all these folks show up, or were they up here the whole time? Doesn't matter. I'm somewhere in the middle of this quiet, sleepy crowd, grasping a printout of my e-ticket for my coach seat tonight. (I have three other copies in my messenger bag just in case this one doesn't work. I swear I'm not paranoid.) There seems to be no real line forming here, just a haphazard swarm of us standing under the platform roof awaiting the signal that we can board.

Naturally, though, we cannot board this train until arriving passengers get off. Somehow we manage to part like the Red Sea to allow the bedraggled folks getting off the train to squeeze past us and head down the stairs into the waiting room. Some of these people are coming from a long way down that platform. I mean, a long, *long* way. Just how big is a train, anyway? I don't think I've ever been this close to a passenger train, except that one time my daughter Addie and I were in London heading to Stratford for the day. Not really the same thing. Plus, I wasn't carrying a bag of anvils and bowling balls like I seem to be doing now.

Once we are given the all-clear to board, I trudge all the way down the platform, with faster passengers passing me up (including some toddlers and the guy with the cane) as if they already know where they're going. I periodically stop to ask an attendant if I am headed in the right direction. One glance at my e-ticket, and I keep getting flagged farther down the platform. I suspect I will end up in Ohio if this keeps up. It would have taken me less time to walk here from home.

Finally I see my coach car and gratefully climb on board. Upstairs, he says? Oh, all right. What's a few more steps at this point? I'll probably have a better view up here anyway. Then I remember this is an overnight trip in the dark and I'm supposed to be sleeping.

The staircase is narrow and winds around on itself up to the second level of the train. There are handrails on both sides, for which I am momentarily grateful until I realize that both hands are full already. The messenger bag keeps getting heavier in my left hand, and the stuffed backpack keeps slipping off my right shoulder, slapping my leg and blocking my way forward and upward. I sense someone right behind me and try to quicken my pace without letting the backpack swing back off my shoulder and into their face. I have never felt more uncoordinated in my life. I hear myself muttering sheepish apologies to whomever is behind me. I don't want to turn around and look, in case it ends up being someone I'm sitting next to all night long. At least the train isn't moving yet. I begin to wonder how I am ever going to move around this bucket of metal once it starts moving if I can't even get up a flight of stairs while it's not.

Somehow my foot finds the top step and I'm on the second level. The car attendant gave me a seat number when I boarded, so I find that aisle seat in the semi-darkness and toss my messenger bag on it. I find a spot in the overhead bin for my backpack... only to discover that I've stuffed the thing so much that it'll never fit up there now. I'm glad I spent all those hundreds of hours on the Amtrak Unlimited forums online for the past six months, because I already know there is a baggage area on the lower level right near the door where we came in. Once everyone passes me and is settled in, I hoist the backpack up again and hurriedly take the thing downstairs to the baggage area. On my way back upstairs, I use both handrails, just for practice. When this train starts moving, I'm going to end up bumping into people left and right, so I might as well get in the habit of grabbing handlebars any time they're offered.

Back in my seat (which now seems spacious without the backpack to worry about), I introduce myself to the woman who is already in the window seat. Her name is Lynda (with the nicer, more exotic spelling of our name) and she's from Michigan. She's also a fellow Taurus, so we get along well. Within that first hour, I tell her my life story even though she hasn't asked, and I realize I'm entirely too keyed up. Folks on all sides of me are rudely trying to sleep or something.

The train motion feels strange. Not like a car, or a plane, or a bus. It has its own rhythm and cadence, and I quickly decide that I like it. But it's going a lot faster than I would have anticipated. Or, at least, it feels like it's going fast. Hard to tell in the dark. I try looking past Lynda out the window and see familiar sights. Of course I do. I live two blocks from these train tracks up in New Brighton, and my car trips to get to the station followed Ohio River Boulevard, which runs parallel a few feet from these tracks all the way downtown. So, essentially, I had to pass all these tracks to get to the station tonight, so I could get on a train to take me back past all these same tracks for nearly the first hour. Even though Lynda hasn't asked, I start pointing out upcoming landmarks and stop only when I realize I'm including things like familiar gas stations and dry cleaners. No wonder everyone else around me is snoring.

I finally make myself shut up after about forty-five minutes of movement, once we have passed my house and I feel I am finally on my big trip for sure. I apologize to Lynda and settle in for what I already know is going to be a crappy night of sleep.

I open the messenger bag as quietly as I can and fidget around for the inflatable neck pillow I purchased just for this trip. I've never used one of these gadgets before, so I'm pretty excited to see how they work. I purchased this particular neck pillow on the recommendation of a friend, and the reviews were stellar, bestowing praise on it for the ease with which you can blow it up without getting winded. I blow into the little nozzle two or three times and it seems to be the size I want.

Beside me, Lynda asks if I'm all right.

"I'm fine. Just blowing up my neck pillow. Why?"

"Oh. I thought you were having an asthma attack."

Apparently I'm not as good at this as I thought.

Lynda adjusts her own neck pillow and leans against the window. I'm on the aisle, so I don't have much to lean against. These seats recline quite a bit, though, and a recliner-like footrest makes the seats even more comfy. But of course, figuring out how to actually raise the footrest is a college course in engineering. And I was an English major. And it's dark. And I'm hyped up on caffeine and adrenaline. And I've got this big inflated pillow around my neck that keeps getting in the way of trying to see what the hell I'm doing.

Somehow I press the right combination of buttons and push back just enough that the footrest finally comes up. I again adjust the neck pillow, which has moved halfway around my neck in the wrong direction, making it look like I'm being mauled by a small pool raft. Sighing, I lean back and close my eyes. But there are too many strange noises on all sides of me, along with the noise of the moving train itself. Large men behind me are snoring loudly, and they don't sound like Wayne so I keep noticing their snores. They're probably faking it and just trying to get back at me for that first hour when I wouldn't shut up about the exciting shopping malls we were passing by.

3:00 a.m.

I've settled in a little better but I'm still not really sleeping. I find myself nodding off periodically but then startling awake when the train shifts funny. And, apparently, trains always shift funny. I'm going to have to get used to this if I want to get any sleep at all on this trip. I look around me and see someone staring at me from between the two seats right in front of us. Someone who looks blue. No, I don't mean sad. I mean blue. And, well, furry. In this light, it's hard to tell for sure, so I lean forward a little bit, hoping to intimidate whoever this is.

Then I realize it's a big blue teddy bear. The guy in the seat in front of Lynda is using a large blue teddy bear with googly eyes as a sort of pillow, and he's got it facing backwards. It's peeking between the seats right at me. Great. This is really going to help me sleep.

4:00 a.m.

I have to pee. I suspect this is going to be a problem, my tiny, spastic bladder. But there's no help for it. I'm going to have to brave these bathrooms for the next few weeks, so I might as well get the first time over with. I head downstairs where there are several bathroom stalls, and I find they're about the size of an airplane bathroom. Maybe a bit bigger. I quadruple-check to make sure I have secured the lock properly and tend to my business. The sink works by pressing down on a tiny faucet handle, and the thing spurts out water like a pressure washer. The front of my shirt gets sprayed, but somehow I get my hands washed, rinsed, and dried without completely drenching myself. The train shifts again just as I'm about to open the door, and I bang up against the side of the wall. The door crashes open and I'm relieved to find I haven't bashed anyone in the face with it. I step into the narrow passage, quietly close the door behind me, and head back upstairs.

At the top of the stairs I notice that the large group of Amish folks who boarded when I did are in this coach car with me. In the last set of seats there is an elderly Amish woman and, I assume, her husband. She's got a neck pillow much like mine, but she's wearing hers backwards. The drop-down tray table attached to the seat in front of her is down, and she's slumped forward completely. The neck pillow is acting like a regular pillow as she snores quietly, her head resting on the tray table. Except for the Amish cap and clothing, I might think she's drunk. I'm pretty sure she's not. Pretty sure.

4:15 a.m.

I'm back at my seat and settled in for the duration. I nod off and wake up about every twenty to thirty minutes until we arrive in Chicago a little after 9:30 a.m. I've slept poorly, I'm cranky, every part of my body hurts from trying to sleep at unnatural angles, and, generally, I feel like I've been hit by a... well, you get the idea.

Day Two

May 2, 2017

10:00 a.m.

I'm inside Chicago's beautiful Union Station. It's a dreary, rainy day so, even though I have nearly five hours to kill till my next train, I have no inclination to venture outside to see the sights. I'm grouchy and tired, and I wish this main waiting room wasn't so historically quaint and lovely (meaning that the seats, though gorgeous, look like stern wooden pews from a Presbyterian church a few centuries ago). Not exactly the sort of spot I'll be able to curl up and catch a few winks this morning.

Plus, I'm hungry and have no idea if I passed a food court on my way here from the platform. There have to be places to eat in this huge building, right? Tell me I didn't walk that twenty miles up the platform from the back of the train (okay, so it wasn't really twenty miles, but just felt like it because I'm tired and famished and confused and lonely and… where was I going with this?) just to get inside the station and find out there's no place to eat for the next five hours.

I sit on one of the completely uncomfortable pews, with my backpack and messenger bag alongside me, unsure what to do. I don't have the energy to walk back down the way I came in, hoping I just walked past some turnoff into a food court. The fact that I have to lug these two bags around with me wherever I go isn't helping my outlook right now. Somewhere in this huge place there are probably lockers I could stuff these bags into, but I don't even want to hunt down someone in charge to ask. I just want breakfast to appear right in front of me right now—some nice, hot scrambled eggs and a big cup of good coffee. Looking around me one more time, I don't see an egg in sight.

To take my mind off my misery, I find the iconic staircase used in the movie *The Untouchables* and take a few lousy pictures. I find out later that there are two such staircases and nobody's really sure which one was used in the movie. Of course, I'm really sure. It's gotta be the one I didn't take a picture of.

As I sit on this pew bench contemplating the uncomfortable walk I'm eventually going to have to take—bags in tow—to use a restroom, I keep seeing people heading into a separate, private lounge area near where I'm sitting. They pass beyond its glass doors and I see them checking in and then looking instantly rejuvenated. Before I left, I'd read about this place: a magical land of milk and honey and Starbucks coffee and snacks. And Wi-Fi. And comfy chairs.

Calculating how long I'll have to sit here waiting for the Southwest Chief to take me the rest of the way to Kansas

City, I decide it'll be worth the twenty-dollar fee to gain entrance to the wonderland before me. The gatekeeper glances at my driver's license and says simply, "Huh." That can't be good, can it? Turns out he's just noticing my birthday, which is this coming Friday. The same as his. We make some comments about having Cinco de Mayo as a birthday, and he then gets serious and continues my interrogation for admittance. After answering half a million questions about myself and handing over more I.D. than I'd need to gain security clearance at the Pentagon—and paying the twenty bucks—I'm allowed inside.

It's a beautiful, large private lounge, and I can put down my bags in the corner and not have to tote them around. There are about six or seven other people in here with me at the moment. We have our own private restrooms. We have a never-ending flow of Starbucks coffee. And juice. And soda. And other earthly drinkable delights. I dump my backpack in the corner and my messenger bag at one of the pub table seats and make a bee line for the small refrigerator. Inside I find every sugary drink known to mankind. All I want is a bottled water. I have medications to take, and I'm seriously dehydrated. Water? They have everything but water?

I finally give up and take my morning meds and supplements with the coffee. It's harder than I thought to wash down pills with scalding hot coffee, but somehow I manage without burning my tongue like I usually do with Starbucks coffee. This is one reason I so rarely drink Starbucks coffee. I cannot be trusted not to sear my own tongue.

Now it's near noon and I'm hepped up on strong coffee and haven't had a decent meal since last night at Eat'n Park with Fara and Emily. My poor diabetic self is crying out, "What are you doing to us, woman? Grab a snack!"

I hate when I yell at myself, so I head over to the snack counter and snatch a little bag of mini-pretzels, which are yummy, and some biscotto, which I accidentally hold in the coffee a little too long and watch it dissolve into a pathetic piece of mush. Delicious mush, though, at least.

I rifle through my messenger bag and dig out the laptop and cord. The pub tables have outlets right on top of them, so I figure I'll update Facebook and Indiegogo and see if the world as I know it has ended since I boarded the train last night. First, though, I have to climb up onto this chair. I don't know who invented pub-height tables and chairs, but it had to be someone with a grudge against short people. I haven't had enough sleep to climb onto this chair in a ladylike fashion. Or a graceful fashion. Or even a remotely human fashion.

But once I put one foot onto the rung of this chair and try to hoist myself onto the seat without pitching off the other side, I realize I can't change my mind and pack everything up and go elsewhere. For one thing, there really aren't any other tables or desks in here. There are a lot of low, comfy armchairs and end tables but nowhere else to sit and properly work on a computer.

Yes, I know they're called laptops for a reason, but the last place I want to perch this thing is on my lap. And now it's a matter of personal pride. I'm not going to let a chair on stilts get the better of me. I'm relieved to find that there are still only a handful of people in the entire lounge and that I'm the only one claiming space at this high table. So I pull myself up onto the chair and grab the table with both hands so I can turn myself facing front. Whew! I'm in the seat now, facing the right direction, and can now plug in the laptop and get to work. And here I thought I wasn't going to get much exercise on this trip.

By the time we're ready to board the train in mid-afternoon, I've had one cup of Starbucks coffee, one cup of decaf, one package of mini-pretzels, one biscotto, a twelve-ounce can of sparkling lemonade, and one of the granola bars I packed in a large pocket of the messenger bag. No protein. Nothing with any solid nutrients in it. Too many carbs, and yet too little of just about everything else. My heart is still pounding from the Starbucks coffee. I'm having fever daydreams about a real meal in the café car of the train.

We are finally called to board, and I try not to look overly anxious as I pack up the laptop and cord and stuff them into the messenger bag. I grab my backpack out of the corner and follow the lounge attendant in order to be sure I get on the right train. (With my luck, I'd stop paying attention at just the wrong moment and end up on a train back east by accident.)

I'm still in coach for this leg of the trip, so I have no privacy to speak of yet. Once I get to the right coach car—which is the very last car of the train, *of course*—one conductor tells us there are no assigned seats. But an attendant inside the train says there are assigned seats. Since nobody's listening to this second guy, and since none of us actually has a seat number, we all spread out around the car. I feel like a rebel. Then I realize it's a good thing I'm taking this trip if sitting in an unassigned seat on public transportation makes me feel like a rebel. How did I get to be this old without pushing the envelope a little bit more than this?

Most of us in this car currently have two seats to ourselves, so I can stuff my gear onto the other seat and relax in this one. The train starts moving—that familiar feeling I've now come to appreciate and love—and I don't wait long before I traipse three or four cars ahead of me and down one level to the café car to get a meal. The tiny "store" area where you pick out your food and drinks is what a typical convenience store would look like if you had to stuff it all into a closet in your hallway. There's a sign just outside saying that only three people are allowed in here at one time. I find that a bit optimistic, by about two people. Still, when it's my turn, I venture in, hoping there is some sort of emergency exit I can't see from my vantage point here near the juices and sodas. I say a quick prayer that the other two people in here with me have showered recently.

On the sage advice of friend and train expert Jenn, who answered some really stupid questions I kept asking her in the months leading up to this trip, I choose a Hebrew National hot dog and pair it with a bag of Lay's potato chips and—glory of glories!—a large bottled water. The café car attendant nukes the hot dog while he's ringing up my order. I pay $9.50 for the large hot dog, the chips, and the bottled water. I'm so hungry for any sort of normal food that I'd gladly pay three times that just to take this humble meal out of this cigar box and back to my seat.

Jenn was right. The Hebrew National hot dog, despite having been nuked in a microwave, is wonderful. I instantly start to feel my blood sugar recovering and my blood pressure and anxiety levels going down. Maybe I can get through this part of the trip after all.

I settle in for the remaining seven hours till I'm in Kansas City, where I'll spend the next two days with my childhood school friend, Sarah. Outside it's still overcast and cloudy. The weather's been either rain or clouds since before I got on the train last night. But, by week's end I'll be in legendary Los Angeles, land of sunshine and beautiful weather. Right now, though, all I can think of is that I desperately want to shower, wash my hair, brush my teeth, and sleep in a real bed.

4:30 p.m.

Out come the ear buds and my Kindle Fire tablet, onto which I've previously loaded a bunch of movies and TV episodes. For the next few hours I watch *Wonder Boys*, a movie I know by heart but which feels so familiar and comforting that I relax still further. When it's over, I pack up the whole messenger bag and head for the observation car, also known as the lounge car. I get out my little notebook and my Alphasmart Neo and transcribe the handwritten notes from yesterday and earlier today before typing new observations directly into the Neo.

The views around me from this car are astounding. Who knew that running the windows up to the roof of this car, and then halfway across the top would give passengers an odd sense of being out in the open? Of course, I'm sitting here on this train, somewhere in Indiana, as far as I can tell, which is a lot flatter than points farther west. The sense of openness might diminish once we're in the middle of the mountains a few days from now.

There are two Amish couples sitting at the table next to mine playing cards. I'm unsure if any of them got on the Capitol Limited with me back in Pittsburgh, or if they got on the Southwest Chief with me in Chicago, or if they were already on the train when I got on a little while ago. Their clothes look familiar, but I'm still not sure. No matter. I'm getting the distinct impression that the Amish really like to ride trains. Either that or they're following me. If they're following me, they have some serious stealth issues. If they merely enjoy train travel as a faster way to get somewhere distant than the horses and buggies, I can't say I blame them. It's certainly a charming way to travel. And except for the major issues with sleep, food, and personal hygiene, so far I'm having a blast.

The card-playing Amish folks are switching from English to whatever that hybrid German is. Is that what we used to call Pennsylvania Dutch? I'm not sure. Plus, we're not in Pennsylvania and they're not Dutch. It occurs to me that they may have started out with me in Pennsylvania and that the "Dutch" is probably a poor mistranslation of *Deutsch*, which does mean German.

I knew those five years of German in school would come in handy.

One table over from the two Amish couples are some massive, burly men with earrings and shaved heads. The contrast is striking and, okay, I admit it, humorous. If I could get away with taking a picture of this odd group, I would. I'm not sure how easily antagonized these guys would become if I started snapping pictures without asking. Not the burly guys. The Amish folks. I'm already pretty sure the burly guys would kick my ass if I whipped out my camera and started clicking away while giggling. Sometimes I wish I was a little bolder. Or a little stupider.

We just had a brief stop out here in the middle of nowhere. Apparently a train ahead of us had to "clear the tracks," whatever that means. I'm guessing it has something to do with the fact that freight trains typically have the right of way over passenger trains. But I don't see any other train pass us as we sit here for five minutes before we start moving again. Now I'm baffled.

The sun has come out, with only a few clouds scattered around the sky above us. Because of all the rain the past few days, there are huge puddles in the fields around us on both sides of the train. Some are so large they look like ponds. Then again, maybe they are ponds. The only better time of year to take this trip than springtime would have been autumn. I can imagine what changing, crisp autumn leaves would look like from a lounge car. Then again, I'm spending more time watching Amish people play cards and talk funny, so what do I know?

Now that I'll be arriving tonight around ten p.m. and don't have to try to sleep sitting up anymore, I'm enjoying being in coach more than I would have thought. I keep reminding myself that the worst part of my trip, in terms of accommodations, is now over. It was brutal going without needed sleep last night, but I'm still glad I chose coach for this first twenty-four hours. It's saved me a lot of money—money I can use later in the trip, I'm sure. It also gave me that needed perspective on train travel. I wanted to experience a little bit of everything, and so far I already have. If I had to sleep in coach again tonight, I might not be so forgiving of last night's experience. I can remember thinking more than once in the middle of the night, "I'm way too old for this." Perhaps I should start making hash marks in this notebook any time that thought crosses my mind. I have a feeling that wasn't the last time I'll think it.

We crossed a time zone this morning while I was on the Capitol Limited. Before the week is out, I'll be crossing two more. Should be a smooth way to transition from East Coast to West Coast, one time zone at a time over the course of several days. Sure, there's jet lag, but nobody's suffered from train lag. But out here, our phones aren't necessarily updating the time automatically. If I don't remember to keep resetting my phone's clock, I won't know where I am, or when.

Now the Amish card players are speaking English. One of the old women is interjecting with things like, "Hey!" and "You guys!" So now I'm completely confused about every Amish stereotype I have apparently been harboring. Next I'll see one of the men wearing a FitBit.

Another stray thought hits me as I sit here alone among strangers. My husband, Wayne, would hate a trip like this, even for a day. He's 6'4" and casts a large shadow. Everything would be too small for him: the seats, the aisles, the restrooms, the booths here in the lounge car. He'd be all right for a while in a coach seat because it'd remind him of his beloved La-Z-Boy at home. But if he were cooped up in here for as long as I have been already, he'd be ready to head outside and climb on top of one of the cars like something out of a bad western.

Suddenly, as I'm envisioning Wayne as a sort of bull-in-the-china-shop, a short freight train passes us heading in the opposite direction. That answers my question about whether there actually is a second set of tracks alongside us. I could have glanced out a window at any time and seen the tracks down there. But no, I was too busy gobbling down granola bars and gawking at innocent people from quaint religious sects.

I continue trying to write about the hilarious things that are happening to me, but when I'm tired and cranky and stuck in a less-than-optimal situation, nothing's all that funny anymore. I start writing down how worried I am that these notes aren't funny, creating a sort of infinite regression loop of references to how unfunny everything is right now. Boy, I need some sleep.

I'm completely zoned out now and have lost track of time. I have no idea where we are on the map. I only know we're no longer in Chicago and we're not yet in Kansas City. That doesn't exactly narrow it down. There aren't any roads out here. Just random brush and trees on either side of us, plus swampy areas from all the rain. No, wait, maybe that was a creek. I look a little more closely. Nope. Swamp. Either way, it's a lot of water. Wait wait wait... no, it's a lake. Nobody builds a dock on the edge of a rain puddle, no matter how big it is or how much rain they're calling for.

6:30 p.m.

I get quite an upper body workout walking from the lounge car back to my coach seat with this heavy messenger bag. Once back at my seat, I discover there is another seat flag next to mine above the seats, and although there isn't currently anyone in this other seat, I notice also that I'm the only one around with two seat flags. That should mean another person will show up and sit next to me at some point. But what do I know? I can't even count how many sets of tracks there are, and I can't tell the difference between a puddle and a lake.

We come to a stop at Fort Madison. This would explain why the train has been slowing down the past few minutes. I'm still not sure where Fort Madison is, but the cars in the station parking lot all have Illinois or Iowa license plates. Plus, "Fort Madison" sounds very midwestern. I'll leave it at that.

We aren't here long—just long enough for passengers to get off or to board. I muse over the fact that the only place I have had to show any identification so far has been to get into the Legacy Lounge in Chicago this morning. In our current times, I find this a tad unsettling, but since my wallet and paperwork have fallen into the trap door of Messenger Bag Hell, it's just as well. The differences between plane and train travel continue to amaze me. Then again, it'd be quite a trick for terrorists to hijack a train and take it to Cuba or something. Pretty sure that would make the evening news. Pretty sure.

12:00 midnight

I'm safely delivered to my friend Sarah's house. She and her little granddaughter Mya met me at the station. I had climbed off the train, out of that very last coach car, and was heading up the long, long platform with the messenger bag and the backpack, and I looked up to see them both coming toward me. I can't remember the last time I was so happy to see a familiar face. At Sarah's house I'm given a partial tour since some of the family are already in bed. None of it is sinking in except when Sarah points out where I'll be sleeping. Then I perk right up. A bed. A real bed. Oh, and what's this down the hall a few steps? A full-sized bathroom with a full-sized shower and everything? Yes, please!

We'll visit more tomorrow. Right now I'm coveting that shower, so I grab my shampoo, soap, toothpaste, and toothbrush and head off for a glorious hot shower and about a half hour of tooth-brushing. I throw on the T-shirt and shorts I've packed for bedtimes, and I'm pretty sure I'm asleep before my head hits the pillow.

Day Three

May 3, 2017

I'm staying in Tyler's room. Tyler is Kristin's nine-year-old son and Sarah's grandson. Seems I've got a pen pal while I'm here. He left me a note welcoming me to his football-themed room. Sitting next to the note on the night stand are two slim hardcover sports-related books he's written and made himself.

Hello my name is Tyler and sorry about the mess. I heard you were an athor and if you look you'll see my books. I have some books I have published.

Response:

Since he has left me a big space to respond, I write a note back thanking him. It's kinda fun to write to the grandchild of a childhood friend.

Hi, Tyler! Your books are wonderful! Treasure them always! You put a lot of work into them.

Thank you for letting me take over your room for two days. I am very glad to have a nice, normal room to sleep in. Sleeping in a seat on the train was a lot harder than I thought it would be. Thanks so much!

Linda M. Au

And I wish I could tell him just how sincerely I mean that note of thanks, because I slept like the dead last night. I woke up in almost the same position I went to sleep. A full eight hours of glorious, uninterrupted sleep. And the bed wasn't moving. At all. Glorious.

After a late breakfast of scrambled eggs, Sarah takes me on a little tour of her fair city. She's pointing out spots that have previously been in the news. One is a spot where a mass murderer shot a bunch of people. Lovely. Another is where a walkway collapsed and killed a bunch of people. Also lovely.

I dub this the Olathe Disaster Tour 2017 and we continue on. I'm not sure Sarah finds this as amusing as I do. I think it's hilarious, but *then again*, I'm still a little punchy. She's the one who has to live here with these cold-blooded murderers and incompetent construction workers. *Then again*, I'm going to board another train tomorrow night—with a boatload of strangers who may or may not want to kill me and throw me off the train in the middle of nowhere. I should know better. I've seen *Strangers on a Train*. This won't necessarily end well. Not that I'm paranoid. Okay, maybe a little. *Then again*, I've also seen *Throw Momma from the Train*. And now I'm glad I didn't invite any of my kids on this trip. No, that's more paranoia talking. Maybe I didn't get enough sleep last night. *Then again*, I've also seen *Silver Streak*. I just hope that the train I'm on next week when we head back to Chicago doesn't go careening off the platform and into Union Station like the Silver Streak does in the movie. That could never happen in real life, right? Either way, I'm glad I have a few pictures of what Union Station looked like before that happens next week.

Okay, that's definitely paranoia. I gotta stop thinking like this. I am secretly glad I haven't seen *The Taking of Pelham 1, 2, 3*. I start wondering if every train movie involves crashing and death and murder. Suddenly a boring, dull trip where nothing happens doesn't seem so bad. Except that I'll have a harder time writing this book.

It's time for a late lunch, so Sarah takes me to a quaint little shopping mall where we grab lunch at a place call Fritz's. With no hint of irony that this is a train-themed restaurant, Sarah assures me this will be a lot of fun. And, once I point out the large locomotive replica out front, she swears she didn't do this on purpose, and we head inside to our table. The main attraction of this place is difficult to miss. I hear the sounds of tiny trains choo-chooing and look up near the ceiling to see a set of tracks running around the whole place, with little trains chugging hither and yon. These trains aren't just for entertainment. Oh, no. They're carrying your food to your table. The process is automated, so once your tiny train reaches your table, it stops and the basket of food descends along a metal strip at the far side of the table. Once you take it off the platform, it rises back up and scurries away to retrieve another order for another table.

Oh, did I mention that you place your order by picking up an old-fashioned corded phone handset and calling it back to the kitchen? As if the tiny trains weren't awesome enough. Add on a big, black heavy phone like the one my grandmother had, and it's perfection.

I'm enchanted by this process, which is clearly meant as a fun distraction for families with children. We haven't brought either of the children, though. We're just two middle-aged women sitting here eating lunch and trying not to look out of place. Well, Sarah seems fine. I'm the one who feels a little like I'm taking up some other kid's table space. I decide I'm a tourist and therefore entitled to this eating experience as much as the loud local kids at the next table.

The only thought keeping this from being a perfect lunch is that I'm reminded of that odd scene in the Dan Aykroyd and Chevy Chase movie, *Nothing But Trouble,* where this creepy murderous family gathers for dinner with their next victims, and a tiny train scoots around the entire table carrying condiments and food. Relieved we're at least in public—in a mall, for crying out loud—I say a quick prayer and enjoy my food.

And on the way out, I insist on getting a paper engineer's hat usually reserved for the kids. It reminds me of those Burger King paper crowns, but way cooler. Every tourist needs souvenirs, so I don't feel bad about taking one for myself. The local kids can come here any time and get a dumb hat. This is my one and only shot at it. The hat is mine. We head back to Sarah's house in victory.

That evening Sarah's daughter Ally and her family come over for dinner. The girls take over the kitchen while Sarah and I continue to chat. I've already had a few long conversations with Tyler about books he's been reading. The kid's a budding genius, far ahead of his years. We discuss book covers and the use of art to tell a story on the outside of a book before you ever pick it up. He shows me some things about a few book covers that I'd never noticed. Suddenly a nine-year-old has made me feel not very observant. And to think I'm a proofreader, a nitpicker by trade.

Now, I won't say that Sarah is obsessive-compulsive or even a neat freak, but she certainly keeps her house neater than I keep mine. (So does most of America, I'm sure.) In the past she's mentioned washing and drying out her kitchen sink because seeing drops of water in it bothers her. She's been known to move everything off her kitchen counter so the beautiful granite can be seen in all its glory. I can appreciate that, especially after she remodeled her kitchen. It looks gorgeous. I'd want to show it off like that too. But I'm just way too lazy to keep putting away the coffeemaker and the knife board and the napkin holder and the salt-and-pepper shakers and... well, you get the idea. I'm lazy. I like my household contraptions within easy reach at all times.

Because of all this, I get a big kick out of watching Sarah's daughters whirl around her kitchen dirtying every pot and pan to make dinner. Reminds me a little of the Tasmanian Devil cartoons, the way they both zip around out there while Sarah and I sit and gab about old times and catch up on new ones. We've known each other since junior high, traveled to England together in our senior year, and had our firstborn babies a mere twelve days apart. I've kept in touch with Sarah more than any other single person from those early days of adolescence, and the ease with which I've slipped into her family today shows that comfort and familiarity.

When the lasagna roll-ups are finally done, we gather in Sarah's dining room for a wonderful dinner: me, Sarah, Kristin, Tyler, and Mya, and also Ally, her husband Matt, her son Brayden, and Matt's daughter Audrey. Hard to believe Sarah and I weren't much older than Tyler and Brayden when we met. How does she have grandchildren this old? She looks like she could pass herself off as their mother. I look like I could pass myself off as *her* mother.

After dinner, the girls decide we need brownies for dessert. I can't say I disagree with this. They whip up a batch as fast as possible, since it's getting late now and Ally and Matt's kids need to get home and get to bed. They yank the pan out of the oven a little too early and we end up eating warm half-cooked brownies with a spoon. I can't say I disagree with this, either. Half-baked brownies are pretty great.

Once the entire house settles down, Sarah and I catch up some more before I realize I'm wiped out and need to get to sleep. Sarah and Tyler will be abandoning me in the morning: school for Tyler and outside work for Sarah. I'll likely work on my laptop in the kitchen, catching up on Facebook, taking notes for the book, updating the Indiegogo backers, while Kristin works at the other end of the house.

Considering I didn't really do anything strenuous today, and I didn't have to get up with an alarm clock or lose any sleep, I can't believe how exhausted I am. It's the good kind, though. The kind where you don't have to get up with alarm clock or lose any sleep again tomorrow. Life is good.

Indiegogo Update

May 4, 2017

May 4, 2017

Wow, everyone!

I'm currently in Kansas visiting a friend from my school days. The first leg of the trip—from Pittsburgh to here—went as smoothly as could be expected. You know, as long as you factor in leaving Pittsburgh around midnight with more than two dozen Amish folks and assorted other strangers and then trying to sleep in a coach seat with people (who apparently are *not* having trouble sleeping in a coach seat) snoring all around you. Add on the strange and often bumpy movement of the train itself and you've got one bleary-eyed traveler by the time we hit Chicago around nine a.m. (Well, we didn't literally *hit* Chicago—that's something from the movie *Silver Streak*.)

I spent much of the day in the Legacy Club Lounge, pumped up on their free Starbucks coffee, eating random snacks and trying to stay awake and not fall off the tall pub-height chair on which I was precariously perched while catching up on Facebook and emails. (If you got an incoherent email from me on Tuesday, I apologize. I was not in my right mind.)

Then, around three p.m., I boarded the second train of the trip, the Southwest Chief, which took me as far as Kansas City, where I got off for the next two days to stay with my friend Sarah. If my calculations are correct, I fell asleep that night in her house about 2.7 seconds after my head hit the pillow. Someone could have declared me legally dead for the next eight hours.

Tonight I get back on the Southwest Chief, which will, as its name implies, take me into the Southwest. Ahh, but from this point on in the trip, I have roomettes. No more coach seats for me.

For now, I'll keep this update short. I'm scribbling notes for the book everywhere I go, and I'll save the jewels of those notes for the book itself. (Okay, this is partly because I'm still not quite caught up on sleep. Or caffeine.)

My next update will likely not come till I arrive in California this weekend. I sure hope you can stand the wait till then.

Day Four

May 4, 2017

By the time I wake up, Tyler and Sarah have both left for the day. There is another note from Tyler. He keeps leaving me notes in his room, and I keep answering them.

Your welcome its cool that your coming over. I'm making another book. I want to talk about it. And my age is 9. I might look young but I'm not 8 or 7. I'm sorry I couldn't read your books but trust me I will.

Tyler, 9

Response:

Hi again, Tyler!

I will never forget our talks about books, book covers, and reading. My age is 55 (56 tomorrow!). I might look old, but I'm not! :)

Read any of my books when you are ready. They will still be there. In the meantime, read what you love--and always love what you read.

Thanks for the room!

Linda

I shower and make my way to the kitchen with my laptop, where I set up shop on the kitchen table. I can hear Kristin down the hall on the phone, working. I make some scrambled eggs and am soon joined by little Mya, who is three, almost four, and their dog, Chugsy, a sort of pug mutt who is about as charming as a pug mutt needs to be in order to get attention.

I'm not exactly writing the sequel to *A Brief History of Time*. Just catching up on note-taking and Facebook posts, so I am thoroughly entertained by little Mya, who plays in the kitchen alongside me as I work. I wish I'd brought a bigger backpack, because I want to smuggle one of these two kids home with me. The dog would never cut it on the train. The toddler might work, but she's too precocious and would give me away in a second. I'll have to make do with the time I'll get to spend with her the rest of today before I leave.

Later in the day, Tyler is home briefly and then back out with his dad for the evening. Sarah comes home and we all head out to a local barbecue chain called Jack Stack. After all, if I'm going to spend two days in Kansas, the land of corn-fed beef and barbecue, I might as well let the locals show me how it's done.

And I'm not disappointed. Somehow, a dish called "Burnt Ends" is my favorite part of the meal. Afterwards we part ways with Mya and Kristin, so I get my vicarious grandma goodbye hugs from Mya and say farewell.

9:00 p.m.

I'm back at the beautiful Union Station building here in Kansas City, Missouri, awaiting the Southwest Chief, which will take me all the way to Los Angeles in about thirty-five hours. For now, I sit here wondering if every train station is called Union Station. There are three or four of them on my trip alone. This station boasts a gorgeous interior, but the actual waiting room is more of those high-backed wooden pew benches that I experienced in Chicago before buying my way into the cushy Legacy Lounge. I don't have that option here, so I'll settle in for the next few hours and do some people-watching.

There's a man seated across from me who is wearing at least three layers of clothing and is carrying what seems to be everything he owns in several plastic bags and a worn backpack. He is also moaning for no apparent reason. I suspect this is today's version of the folks who rode the rails in lieu of being homeless, though they were stereotypically riding freight trains in all the movies. A few young adults wander in periodically, sporting the latest gear and wearing the latest high-tech sneakers, walking while staring at phone screens.

They're probably on those cool Rail Passes I've seen ads for everywhere. Facebook friends post the links for these deals about every twelve or thirteen hours, ad nauseam. ("See the country for $97 on a Rail Pass!") Nobody seems to realize that your hundred bucks gets you only a seat in coach for three thousand miles or more, but no bed, no food. Just a seat and access to the more public parts of the train. I suppose the young college types can handle this, and would even find it adventurous and glamorous. Me? I'm too old for that shit. (I mentioned being old. Add another hash mark.) Give me a bed and include my meals any day.

Like, for instance, today. I'm now completely past my coach seat "adventure" and will now have roomettes for the rest of my trip. This will mean privacy when I want it, a place to put my gear so I needn't carry it around, an attendant when I feel lazy, a truly horizontal bed when I'm sleepy, and three meals a day in the dining car. No more microwaved hot dogs and potato chips, unless I want them. Now it's tablecloths and real flatware. And beds. Did I mention the beds?

Around 10:15 p.m., I look up from my musing to see a family of Amish people congregating just outside the waiting room. I knew it. I'm being stalked by the Amish. They probably have a hit out on me because my clothing makes them look gaudy.

I knew they were Amish even before I saw their clothing because I caught a glimpse of what they were all carrying. I've noticed this trend with Amish folks who travel. First, they all have wheeled suitcases in unusual patterns: garish floral prints, bold geometric designs, hot pink and neon colors. I wonder if they've found a loophole in their rules about plain clothing. You don't wear a suitcase, so you can buy the craziest patterns and colors you can find. Or do they find these designs cheap because nobody wants to be caught dead with a suitcase sporting huge neon flowers that look like they stepped off a bedspread from the 1970s?

Second, the Amish carry whatever doesn't fit into their suitcases in large, heavy plastic bags. Not trash bags. Not Walmart bags. I'm talking large department store bags from Macy's or J.C. Penney's. The good, sturdy bags you get when you buy, like, $500 worth of clothes. Where do they get these bags? Does Macy's have an Amish Clothing section downstairs that I've been missing all these years? I certainly don't have any of these bags. I never step foot in a Macy's. I can't afford it. Plus, I'm lower than low-maintenance. I'm no-maintenance. If a blouse I bought fifteen years ago still fits and doesn't have ketchup stains on it, it's still in the rotation.

So where did these Amish folks all get their Macy's bags? I saw this family's baggage—the suitcases and the plastic bags—before I saw the people, and I immediately knew they were Amish. Then they stepped into the waiting room and confirmed my predictions. It's a good thing I'm an introvert or I would have embarrassed myself by sauntering up to them and asking how they came into possession of those Macy's bags.

And a second question would definitely have been: What is IN those bags? Are they carrying extra skull caps and black skirts in there? Or more brightly colored shirts and blouses? Another pair of sturdy black New Balance sneakers? I'm so curious I can barely stand it. This is my first indication that I am spending too much time in waiting rooms on this trip.

11:00 p.m.

I'm on board the Southwest Chief, in my very first roomette! It's late at night, so I find my roomette here on the lower level is already made up into a bed. I toss down my bags and sit on the bunk, facing back out into the narrow hallway. With the bed out, the walkable floor space left measures about six inches by two feet. My two feet, that is. And I have small feet. My Sleeping Car Attendant (SCA) comes by to welcome me. His name's José and he'll be on this train with me all the way to Los Angeles. For a moment I think this must be the coolest job in the world. Then I realize he'll have to put up with me and my obnoxious newbie questions for the next thirty-five hours. And not just me. Everybody else in this area, too. Day and night. Now I think this must be the worst job in the world.

José tells me that I don't really have any neighbors at this end of the car right now. I smile politely and thank him, but inside I'm partying like it's 1999. I have not only this whole roomette to myself tonight, but the entire hall! I close the roomette door and start to arrange my belongings. I think I have this disorder that clearly needs its own name and nonprofit foundation. Specifically, I have this uncontrollable urge to personalize any space I occupy for more than eight hours. Kinda the way male dogs lift their legs on trees to mark their territory, only less smelly.

I take out my tech gear and charger cables, cords and books and toiletries, and start to find spots for them around the small room. I'm overly prepared for any eventuality because I've been living on the Amtrak Unlimited forums for months now. I've brought several dozen items that involve Velcro or rubber bands or binder clips, plus adapters and extensions for all sorts of stuff I probably didn't even bring with me. I'm ready for anything.

And I'm all alone. For days.

Until I glance up along the wall near the small mirror and see a fly. A fly. In my room. With me. Seems I'm not alone after all. I unlock and slide open the door and try to shoo him out of the room. Instead, he decides to fly deeper *into* the room, somewhere above my head behind the upper bunk where I can no longer see him. Great. Just what I need.

I go back to my personalizing, hoping to forget he's here. I sit on the bed and change into my T-shirt and shorts and start thinking about sleep. But there is a fly somewhere in this roomette with me. And I'm sure he's a male because women never annoy me this much. Only men.

And, in a space this small, a single fly—male or female—suddenly seems gargantuan. This roomette isn't big enough for both of us, buddy. One of us is going to have to die, and it ain't gonna be me. Then, I see him land on the narrow mirror on the far wall. Remembering that I am cataloguing this entire experience for posterity, I quietly slip my camera out of the messenger bag and snap a few pictures of the fly before slowly leaning down to the floor and picking up one of my cheap flip-flops. In one deft movement that could only have been the hand of God (because I never get this lucky at home), I hit the fly dead center, and his body smooshes onto the mirror and is stuck there. So now I'm sharing my first night in a sleeper car with the rotting corpse of my enemy. And here I thought I'd be traveling alone on this trip.

Still, I fear that there has to be some sort of retribution, divine or otherwise, for starting this leg of my trip with cold-blooded insect murder.

To take my mind off my heinous crime, I take pictures of the room from just about every angle. I've already got a picture of the dead fly on the mirror, so I skip that wall. Really, there aren't that many angles anyway, so this doesn't take long. I slip on the flip-flops, ignoring the fact that one of them probably still has a bit of fly guts on the bottom, and visit the tiny bathroom down the hall before settling in for the night.

The train just blew its whistle, meaning either we're crossing a road somewhere or going through a town—or the engineer just likes to amuse himself by waking us all up at random times during the night. After all, how would we know the difference? It's a lovely sound, though—soothing in its own way, so I don't mind a bit. I live two blocks from tracks like these and hear whistles like this throughout the day and night. Hearing them now while I'm finally on a real train is that much better.

One good thing about traveling alone is that I get to use both pillows in this roomette. And both the blankets if I want them. And both of the bottles of water. I'm a roomette supply hoarder, and I don't care who knows it.

I've got both pillows behind my back right now as I sit here on the bottom bunk with the Alphasmart Neo. After jotting down a bunch of notes on how my day has gone so far, I realize that trying to sit up like this isn't all that comfortable after all. The pillows are too floofy to be back rests. Time to shut this thing down and try to get some sleep. I have a feeling I'll need plenty of rest in order to tackle my first full day of hygiene and meals on a passenger train.

No turning back now.

Day Five

May 5, 2017

I'm awake. It's 7:00 a.m. local time, which is probably still the Central time zone. The time of day has less meaning here than at home. That's probably because I don't have to cook someone else breakfast at six a.m. or head to bed at any certain hour. Or do anything that's part of a typical day.

My first thought is, "So this is what seven a.m. looks like. Huh." My second thought is, "Should I try to get more sleep?" This is a question I ask myself pretty much every morning, but today my answer is different. Nope, I'm going to get up and start my first full day on a long-distance train. It's not like anything monumental is going to happen today. I'm going to be on this train till tomorrow. But it feels like the start of a big adventure. Today is my birthday, and it seems a fitting way to celebrate. I find I'm hungry and ready to make my first trip to the dining car.

But first, a shower.

I can't say I've been looking forward to this part of the trip, but I keep using the word "adventure" and hope it fools me into believing it. I pack up my extremely basic toiletries—trial-size shampoo and soap—and the towels and take the walk down the hall to the shower stalls. Nobody's around, so I go right in. This room is about twice the size of the bathroom, which isn't saying much. A shower curtain and a small lip in the floor separate the room into two sections: the changing area with a small seat, shelf, and mirror, and the shower stall, with another shelf and a drain.

The walls are wet, so someone's been here already, but it's otherwise clean enough. I put the toiletries on the small shelf inside the shower stall and hang up the towels outside the stall near the door.

I quadruple-check the sketchy little untrustworthy lock on the door, to make sure it's securely fastened. Is it wobbling back and forth? I can ill afford to pay for another passenger's emotional therapy should the door swing open into the hallway while I'm showering.

I've showered in a moving cruise ship before, but that movement is a lot more subtle, and those bathrooms are a lot bigger. So, while I try to master the artful dance of showering on a moving train, my brain shuffles through a series of random, yet oddly focused thoughts.

- There aren't enough handrails in this shower. It's moving back and forth, for crying out loud.

- There's a washcloth hanging here that the previous person must have left behind. Let's make sure I don't actually touch it.

- Lord, please don't let me die in here. I can't bear the thought of being found dead in this shower stall.

- There really aren't enough handrails in this shower.

- I remember that my friend Jenn said she was in one of these showers once when the water cut out completely while she still had shampoo in her hair. She had to wait a few hours before she could wash it out. Not only is the water pressure better than our shower at home, but it lasts long enough for me to wash and rinse off completely. I don't care what happens to the next person. At least I got *my* shower.

- Getting underwear and shorts back on while standing in a small puddle is difficult. Getting wet feet through leg holes without soaking the clothing requires enough skill and coordination that it should be an Olympic sporting event. And I wouldn't get even the bronze.

- Lord, seriously, please don't let me die in here.

I am again reminded of how miserable my tall husband would be if he had accompanied me on this trip. He wouldn't have fit in even the bottom bunk in the roomette. He wouldn't appreciate the chrysallis shower stall I just came out of. And he certainly wouldn't want traveling to take this long when it doesn't have to. I'm pretty sure he wouldn't understand the reason I'm on this train in the first place. Which is precisely why I never really tried to explain it to him. Sometimes it's painful watching his brain try to wrap itself around my way of looking at the world.

8:00 a.m.
Breakfast in the Dining Car
Somewhere in Western Kansas

I'm still getting used to doing mostly normal things, such as showering or eating, and not having a clue exactly *where* I'm doing them. Oddly, when I've done these things on a cruise ship, it doesn't occur to me to wonder where I am. That's probably because I'm out in the middle of the ocean and not on terra firma. But right now I'm in some actual state of the union, some part of the United States. I just don't know which one.

Meals are included with sleeper car accommodations, and because sleeper cars are at the same end of the train, those of us with such accommodations enter the dining car from the same door. Coach folks enter from the opposite end and usually are not seated with sleeper car folks unless there are too many more people at one end of the car than the other at any given time. Breakfast and lunch are typically first come, first served, although dinner is usually by reservation.

And this is where the introvert nightmare could start. I come into the dining car and wait at the doorway to be seated. Oh sure, they ask you how many are in your party, and when you say "One," they know they've found another easy victim. The dining car attendants are experts at math. Well, at counting to four, anyway. The goal is to maximize the small amount of space in the dining car by filling up each table. If one party of two comes in, two more people will be seated at their table before they start seating people at the next table. A party of three gets their own table until a lone wolf like me comes along.

When asked, I squeak out the "One" and follow the attendant to my fate. There are already three people at this table so I complete the foursome and sit down. Next to me is a woman from Kansas and across from us is a retired couple heading to the Grand Canyon and then points west after that. I order some simple scrambled eggs and bacon and coffee and listen in on the conversation. I discover later that nearly every dining car conversation starts with talk about Amtrak, then about destinations and reasons for taking the train in the first place. And this first dining car conversation fits neatly into that template. When asked, I mention that this is a bucket-list item and that I'm writing a book about the experience. I hand out three business cards I've made just for this occasion. I feel almost like a professional and not a sham impostor.

Since my three dining companions all have histories in farming, the conversation turns there, brought up naturally by the fact that we are careening headlong through mile after mile of farmland. There's something lovely and romantic (in the traditional sense of the word) about eating a meal in this dining car, with tablecloths and proper flatware, as we wind our way across the country. I don't say a whole lot at breakfast—I'm the only non-farmer in the bunch—but I find I'm enjoying listening to this interesting and pleasant conversation. I keep sipping my coffee slowly in order to give myself something to do while I listen. I don't spill any on myself. Points for me.

Conversation turns to Tom Hanks (as all good conversations do), who apparently says he'd keep Amtrak running and even improve it if he were president. I'm already a fan of Hanks for his love of typewriters (I own about a dozen myself), so hearing this gives me another reason to appreciate him. He understands the need to slow down and pay attention in life, to not always be in a hurry to compute, to rush from place to place, to go digital.

Somehow I manage to get through the entire meal without blurting out that it's my birthday. I'm proud of myself for this small bit of restraint. But the day is young. At home, this is about the time I'd be getting up for the day, and here I am in the middle of the country, showered, dressed, and fed. Anything can still happen between now and bedtime tonight. But right now, I feel like a real grown-up.

9:15 a.m.

I head back to my roomette, feeling as if I have conquered the world simply because I sat with three strangers and ate a meal in front of them without spilling food all over myself. Let's face it: meeting strangers is difficult enough for me. Add on eating a meal with strangers, and it's a recipe for disaster. I still have a lot more meals like this to endure, but this first one has gone better than anticipated. I chalk it up as a win and settle in for a morning of note-taking and farmland-watching from my roomette.

José has made the roomette back into a room. The bed and blankets and sheets are nowhere to be found. I now have two facing seats to myself and can sit forward or backward, as I choose. I still get both the pillows, too, during the day, which is a nice little perk. I love pillows. At home, I collect throw pillows the way some people collect Pokémon.

I unfold the little table and get out my laptop. I'm glad I have a tiny 11″ laptop because this table is a bit teeny. I honestly don't see how two people could use it at the same time, even with small laptops like this one. But since it's just me, I'm golden. As I sit here, though, I notice that, every so often, I get a whiff of what smells like a chemical toilet. Like a port-a-potty might smell when it's fresh. Well, not *fresh.* You know what I mean. It's not overpowering, but it is noticeable. I wonder if I'm going to have to endure this for the next week or if it's a fluke. Of course, now my overthinking brain is also wondering just what happens with all that... *stuff*... during a long-distance train trip like this. Probably best not to think about it too much. Not till after I get home, where we have proper indoor plumbing.

BREAKING NEWS! We recently passed Lamar, Colorado, and we just zipped by George and Nancy Idler's house. I know this because they have a huge carved wooden sign out front for everyone to see. I just thought you'd like to know that. I wave. *Hi, George and Nancy!*

It hasn't even been twelve hours since I boarded, but I'm already enjoying having this small space to myself. It's big enough to be functional, and it gives me a sense of "place," which I'm starting to believe is something I need. I personalize my spaces as soon as I can—which is why I fussed with everything last night before going to sleep—and a sense that a place is mine (even for a short while) seems to be vital for my productivity. I can also work in a library or coffee shop because that small table or space is temporarily mine. I claim it, guard it, and then get to work.

Sometimes I wonder why I've got so many weird quirks. Is this an introvert thing again, or something else? Is this some knee-jerk reaction to bad days in my past where so many things were up-ended or lost—objects, people, relationships? Do I instinctively protect what feels like mine? Wow, I really do need better hobbies. Back to paying attention to the world currently around me...

Because two people in another roomette in this hallway are talking (and coughing), I've given up and put in the ear buds with the tiny clip-on MP3 player. I'm listening to the Beatles' *One* album. I can still hear some of the train track noise underneath it, but that's kinda nice. And having a soundtrack for the trip isn't such a terrible thing.

9:30 a.m. Mountain Time

At some point we shifted to another time zone and are now two hours behind where I started on Monday. Just now, I caught a glimpse of some actual mountains off in the distance. Snow-capped peaks and everything. Huh. Apparently America isn't just one big flat pancake of farmland all the way across. Who knew?

I get a "happy birthday" text from my twentysomething daughter Addie, who asks me to buy her some weed in California. Little does she know that, if I buy weed in California (or Colorado, or anywhere else), it'll be my own private stash. Mommy's under a lot of stress out here with people waiting on her hand and foot, with no laundry or dishes or cooking to do for the next week. Nice try, though.

I continue to take pictures through these windows in the roomette, which aren't the cleanest windows in the world. Upon the advice of experts in the Amtrak Unlimited forum, I packed a small spritz bottle of glass cleaner and have already cleaned the inside of the windows. There's no help for the outside, though.

Should I take pictures every time those mountains look a little bit bigger? Why not? I've got room on the camera card. *Click. Click.* These are going to look really unimpressive and boring on Facebook later.

10:23 a.m.

The conductor just came on the P.A. system saying someone had been smoking in one of the restrooms. He gives a gentle (read: not so gentle) reminder that anyone caught smoking on board the train will be removed by local law enforcement. No exceptions. There's my morning's bit of excitement, I suppose. Shaming the smokers into diving off the train at the next stop.

Every so often, especially if we're moving slowly in or out of a station, I feel as if I'm on an amusement park train ride for kids. The sounds are the same; the rocking is the same. And, to be honest, that's the only previous train experience I have except for heading to Stratford with Addie in England in 2008, though that was more like a large commuter train than a long-distance passenger train. Still, I enjoy the sensation of feeling like a little kid for a while.

11:21 a.m.

We're in our first tunnel. It's pitch black outside the windows, though I can see with the light from my laptop, and there are lights in the hallways I hadn't noticed till now. I wouldn't have expected it to be quite this dark out there. This isn't anything like the Fort Pitt Tunnel or Squirrel Hill Tunnel in Pittsburgh. It's possible to get all the way through those and forget to turn your headlights on. Here, it's a bit unnerving to look out these windows and see absolutely nothing, knowing we're still careening rapidly forward. The engineer can see in front of him, right? The headlights are on, right?

Back out in the open countryside, I see a lot of sets of what are almost surely horse hoofprints alongside the tracks as we ride slowly along. Wonder what sorts of people are riding right along these tracks. Are they riding for fun? For work? Or something in between?

You know you're in the middle of nowhere when there aren't even power lines running alongside the tracks. Or, at least, not on this side of the train. In spots like this one, with no other signs of civilization except the train tracks and the very occasional power lines, I wonder how tenuously those power lines keep civilization flowing into the small towns I see every so often.

The dining car attendant just came around to everyone—sleeper passengers first—to take lunch and dinner reservations. I have a 1:15 reservation for lunch and a 6:15 reservation for dinner. We'll see who I'm sitting with once I get there. I almost hope it's some of the folks here in my corridor. It would make passing them every hour or two in order to pee a little more cordial. I hate to think all these people know about me is that I have a really tiny bladder.

Parts of the scenery remind me of video games: specifically, Minecraft and Obduction. I can't wait to get home and start a new Minecraft world and see if it looks like New Mexico. My gosh, I am such a nerd.

11:40 a.m.
Raton, New Mexico

This is a quick, literally five-minute stop. Judging from how many pictures I've seen online of this station from many other train passengers, though, I'm guessing it's often a much longer stop. But we're about an hour behind schedule, so I suspect they're making up a bit of time here and points forward.

We're told there are no other step-off-the-train stops (a.k.a. "smoke break stops") until Albuquerque, sometime around five p.m. today. Frankly, I'm surprised that we're in New Mexico already, and that we'll still be in New Mexico five hours from now.

11:51 a.m.

That moment when you see a Winnebago in New Mexico and wonder if the local crystal meth is any good...

I've been staring out this window at what might seem the same view for a while now. And I was rewarded with the sight of several prairie dogs scurrying around their mounds outside the train in the brush. I've always had a fondness for prairie dogs and used to hover around their enclosure at the Pittsburgh Zoo any time we took the kids there. This is the first time I've seen them out in the wild instead of inside a zoo. I'm briefly surprised that they don't look any different.

12:00 noon

Where the Deer and the Antelope Play (and the cows and the horses and the humans on smoke break)

The wildlife continues to fascinate me. You'd think that a huge, hulking piece of loud metal whooshing by you, making all sorts of racket, would warn you to steer clear. But I guess these guys get used to the trains, like the semi-tame squirrels and bunnies and cardinals and ground hogs in my backyard have gotten used to hearing me chatter at them as I feed them. Not that we're feeding the antelope bounding across the plains right outside my window. Wish I knew exactly what they are. The best I can do is say they're the kind with the big white butts. I'll figure out later what kind they are. It's unfortunate for them that they have those big white butts. Otherwise they'd blend in well and I might not have seen them.

12:35 p.m.

There are more antelope alongside the train. Poor things must have missed the last stop. Faster, you idiots! Faster! Your big white butts are giving you away! Great, now I'm talking to wild animals through the windows of a moving train. I probably could use more sleep.

12:56 p.m.

An extremely large hawk flew alongside the train for a while. Should have gotten a picture, but I was too busy hawk-gawking and enjoying the view. I must say, I'm surprised at all the wildlife that seems to hover around a passing train. If I were a piece of wildlife (and I wasn't, even when I was younger), I'm not sure I'd get this close to a train. Still, I'm not complaining. It's like going to the zoo, without the smell. I suddenly get another quick whiff of the chemical toilet down the hall. Never mind. It's a lot like going to the zoo. It just costs a lot more.

1:15 p.m.
Lunch in the Dining Car

The attendant seats me with a man probably in his mid-thirties. Just the two of us. Evidentally this attendant cannot count to four. Joy of joys. Just when I was getting used to sitting with three other people and quietly blending in, and realizing it didn't have to be uncomfortable, I sit alone at a table with a man not much older than my first-born son. Yeah, this isn't going to be weird at all.

There is naturally a bit of awkwardness as we talk. I'm infinitely grateful that at least we have a passing view to stare at outside the window. If the train weren't moving, it would be weird to stare out a window rather than look at one's lunch companion, but a lot of folks look out the windows while in the dining car. However, we do have to speak to one another at least a little bit, just to be civil and normal, even if I suspect he is not completely normal. I'm sensing his social skills are a tad off, though I'm no shining conversationalist right now, either. He tells me he's from Michigan—and New Jersey, originally. I nod a lot. That helps.

I have the quesadillas for lunch. They aren't too bad—and not heavy, either. Just right for lunch. I start to feel as if I might eat fairly healthy on this trip after all. Then I go and ruin it by having dessert, but it was yummy and it's my birthday and nobody's gonna make me a birthday cake out here in the desert, so I'm not going to feel too bad about it. (It was a tiny chocolate Bundt cake with pecans on top and a caramel center… with a single strawberry on the side. Happy birthday to me.)

My lunch companion and I talk a lot about the scenery out the window. (Thank God for scenery out the window.)

Right now we're still in New Mexico, so we see lots of sage brush, red clay, and old dry-rotted rubber tires in their natural habitat. At least this makes for more interesting conversation between us. Okay, so not actually *interesting*... just slightly more interesting than when we were staring out the window. At some point we discover the natural conversation filler of *Monty Python and the Holy Grail* quotes, and I relax a little bit.

We see two possibly wild burros while we're eating. One's white, and the other one's brown. I hope they're wild because if they belong to someone, they are seriously lost. "Hey, Carl, where the heck is the food trough? We've been walking for hours. I think we passed this same tumbleweed an hour ago."

I make it through lunch without mentioning that it's my birthday. I'm two for two and ridiculously proud of myself for no apparent reason.

After lunch, back in my room—after I realize I didn't ask my companion's name—I see a recliner chair sitting out in the middle of the brush. All by itself, with no houses around. I can't begin to imagine how it got out here. Or why. But I'm pretty sure I want to know. "Hey, George, the Barco-lounger busted. Can we throw it on yer truck and dump it out off Route 27 up the road a piece? You know, way out near the train tracks where nobody will see it..."

I'm noticing that there'll be lots of nothing as far as the eye can see—just brush and empty land—then suddenly there are a few trailer homes or one lone farm building. All alone out here. It makes me wonder how those people get onto the power grid. And I wonder where they go grocery shopping. Or get gas for their vehicles. My nameless lunch companion noticed solar panels at one such location, so that might explain it. Add a propane tank or two and you're all set. Except for the grocery thing. And the gas. And the non-existent Wi-Fi. I could never live out here. I need my internet. No Netflix, no peace.

Now I'm back in my room, with the door closed (which seems to help not only with noise but with the chemical smell), taking notes, with my feet up on the edge of the seat across from me. I am sad this portion of the trip ends tomorrow morning already, but now I anticipate that long stretch on the Zephyr once I'm heading back east next Tuesday. I'll get one daytime day trip on the Coast Starlight next Monday—about twelve hours, morning to evening—in order to get north from Los Angeles to Emeryville where I can get on the Zephyr. I've got a roomette for that day trip, too. At first it seemed a tad extravagant for a daytime trip that won't involve sleeping, but I'll like having the privacy, I think.

Gazing out the window again as I daydream, I wonder, what are the purple flowers springing up in many spots alongside the tracks? They're the only color added to the landscape besides greens and browns. They're obviously hardy stuff to be growing so lush in such an area. They're growing almost like ground cover. Just past Lamy, New Mexico, I see some scrub flowers again, only in bright red this time. I can't get over how stunning this splash of color looks in this arid area. I might have to be serious for a few moments in order to appreciate it.

It's funny, but we slow down to a crawl at the oddest times. I suspect that a lot of it now is because of curves in the tracks. A big ol' train can't just take the turns at top speed.

We're snaking through various shallow canyons, and I'm sure a train this heavy needs to take such turns at ridiculously slow speeds. Sometimes I bet I could jog alongside the train and keep up. Now there's a sight nobody wants to see. Especially me because it would mean, like, exercise.

I admit to a childlike glee when the train has to make these slow curves. My sleeper car is just far enough back (though still quite near the front of the train) that when the train is banking a curve like this, I can see the engine and the first cars clearly from my window. I don't know why I find this fascinating. I just do. I'm easy to please.

The slow pace gives my brain time to wind down a bit, too, so I can muse over the many small observations I keep making as we travel west.

For one thing, when I was in coach, I liked bagging up my entire messenger bag (since I wasn't about to leave precious electronics at my unguarded seat) and heading to the lounge car/observation car/café car. (Those terms are largely interchangeable.) That vantage point gave me a nice view plus a table to sit and use the Alphasmart or laptop. Today, my first full day in a sleeper car, I haven't felt much of a desire to go to the observation car.

I think I'll save that experience for the Zephyr and its amazing views. The view out my roomette window is pretty great, though I can see only on one side of the train, of course. Sure, I'm seeing burros and hawks and antelope and La-Z-Boys out this side, but there could be an entire town on the other side. That would make the wildlife a lot less wild, but it would probably explain the La-Z-Boy.

What seems different is that I feel perfectly comfortable and spoiled here in my own private area. I can do the socializing thing at meals—in fact, I'm kinda forced to—but then I can come back here and still have a great view and a comfy chair and table to work on. And, you know, no other people.

Of course, part of the comfy-table part is that I brought a small laptop that actually fits on this small table, and I'm short enough to be able to sit in these chairs and not feel as if I have to hunch over to type.

Random question: How do they calculate how high something is above sea level if it's this far from the actual sea?

4:30 p.m.

Another announcement comes over the P.A. system, this time announcing that the toilets in the last two coach cars are not working. They are clogged. Whichever poor shmoe has to make these announcements says calmly but with a certain edge in her voice: "Please watch what you put in the toilets. Someone put paper towels in the toilets and clogged them. Don't put paper towels in the toilets." Things that seem obvious to me as someone who raised four children are apparently not as obvious to other people. The quality of people in coach has really gone downhill since Monday night. Location, location, location.

I love how all the announcements seem to have a chastising and shaming quality to them. I feel like we're being rapped on the proverbial knuckles by a mean hall monitor. Hey, lady, it wasn't me, so back off. I briefly wonder where all those people in coach are going to go to the bathroom. I decide not to complain about the faint chemical toilet smell at this end of the train. Seems it could be worse.

I glance out the window to try to dispel the image of many clogged toilets at the other end of the train. I see some rundown houses with piles of tires, old rusted cars, stacks of wooden pallets, and wait... Is that a sweat lodge?

Just when you thought you'd seen it all.

5:20 p.m.

We've got a smoke break stop of about a half hour. Some folks had five o'clock dinner reservations and are presumably sitting in the dining car, eating, while the train is stopped. What a great view they have while eating: a rail yard. Frankly, I'm surprised this didn't happen to me. It's the kind of thing that would. Then again, it's still my birthday, so I'm still entitled to a few more good things today.

This is also a maintenance stop, so I watch a window washer outside our windows. He's got a lot of windows to cover in this short amount of time so he's really hustling. Once he's done, the streaks on the outside of the windows will now be going in the opposite direction in brand new spots. Just when I thought I had figured out where to point my camera out the window to avoid blurry pictures.

I restrain myself enough to avoid writing "You missed a spot" on a Post-it note and sticking it to the window. I'm sure he's never heard that joke before. Besides, I'm above that sort of cheap, obvious, overdone humor.

6:15 p.m.
Dinner in the Dining Car

I am seated with the same young man I ate lunch with. Again. Just the two of us. Again. Suddenly I'm wishing for more people at the table, which isn't very introverted of me. We'd exhausted the usual awkward conversation topics at lunch, assuming we were parting ways forever. If I had known I'd have to spend another whole meal alone with him, I would have held off talking about the solar panels or the old tires outside the window. You know, saved some interesting topics for later.

Turns out, we hadn't discussed where either of us was heading, so I'm relieved to have some sort of normal topic to cling to. Mr. Thirtysomething is headed to Flagstaff to a friend's wedding and will be getting off the train later tonight after dark. Is it wrong that my first thought is relief that I won't be having breakfast with him? I'm too married and too old (another hash mark for me) to have exciting, private conversations on a train with men young enough (and weird enough) to be my son.

I choose the chicken carbonara fettucine, which comes with a vegetable medley. It is surprisingly good, and although I'm not sure I'm all that hungry, I eat nearly all of it. Plus dessert. Remember, *birthday*.

At a conversation lull, I break down and mention that it's my birthday and otherwise ruin my perfect record of keeping my mouth shut about it. He wishes me an obligatory happy birthday and, to my relief, doesn't ask how old I am. (Hash mark.) I probably would have told him anyway. It was just that kind of conversation.

7:20 p.m.

The train is at least an hour behind schedule, probably more. I'm not sure if we'll be able to make up the time now that there aren't many stops left before Los Angeles in the morning. Of course, the night owl in me won't be upset if we get in a little later tomorrow morning. It'll make it easier to get up, dressed, and off the train in one piece. I suspect it'll be a bit hectic anyway, so having to do it a little later in the morning is fine. I still wish mornings started around noon.

Right now, the tracks are in the middle of a huge flat plain, with striking mountains rising up on all sides of us. Obviously it's easier for trains to travel on flat terrain, and that'd be why the tracks are here. But it sure makes for interesting scenery all around us. We're also getting closer to sunset so the lighting has changed, both inside and outside the train. I hope I'll get a good view of a postcard sunset. Of course, the pictures will suck and won't do it justice, but at least I'll be able to see it live, in person.

9:00 p.m.

The sun's gone down over wherever we currently are. José has just asked me when I want the bed made up, so I randomly say 10:30 but add that it can be anytime in that general area. I should have said 10:37, just to see his reaction. I think I'll whip out the Kindle and do a little reading. I must admit, sitting on a moving train in a private little room, reading after dark, is pretty terrific. Have I mentioned I'm really low maintenance?

11:00 p.m.

José has come and magically turned my little room into a little bedroom again—the way I found it last night when I got on the train in Kansas City. I stood outside in the narrow hallway watching him deftly pull down the bunk to get the sheets and blanket, then zap it closed again, pull my two seats together into a bed, and then whip all the sheets and the blanket into place. The man's got some mad bedmaking skillz. I bet he can fold a fitted sheet blindfolded, too. I find this strangely attractive in a man.

Time to shut down the brain for the night. The train movement in the dark is lulling me to sleep.

Day Six

May 6, 2017

7:00 a.m.
Somewhere in California

It's 7:00 a.m.

My phone says 8:00 a.m.

My body says 10:00 a.m.

This is the only day I can manage to be a morning person: when I cross time zones heading west on a train and can trick my brain into thinking it's still ten o'clock and not seven o'clock. Tomorrow, though, all bets are off.

I'm not clear on when we expect to arrive at (another) Union Station in Los Angeles, but it clearly won't be the 8:15 a.m. projected time on my e-ticket. I decide to get dressed and go have another adventurous breakfast that I don't have to cook or clean up after. I find that getting dressed here in the roomette isn't a whole lot easier than getting dressed in the shower stall. Sure, my clothes won't get wet (unless that tiny bladder decides to give out on me), but since this is still a bedroom until I leave and allow José some space to presto-change-o this back into a sitting room, there is essentially no floor space. So I have to sit or lie on the bed and get dressed, while the train continues to bump along. How I'll end this trip without multiple bruises and contusions is beyond me.

Once dressed I sit on the bed for a few more minutes and see what has changed outside my window since last night. We're finally back in civilization, in a somewhat urban area. As seems to be typical of so many areas around train tracks in a city, we're passing the poorer sections of town. These areas aren't meant to lure potential passengers with the exotic romance of train travel. And there's really nothing funny about them for me to write about, either.

7:45 a.m.
Breakfast in the Dining Car

I have breakfast in the dining car again, this time seated with people I will promptly forget once I get back to my room. It's not their fault. My brain has figured out that it's before eight a.m. and that, if I were back home at this hour, I'd still be sleeping. I am therefore focusing entirely on the really good coffee. I define "good coffee" as "coffee prepared the way I like it." I am no coffee snob, unless you mean I become a snob if I don't get my coffee. I eat my scrambled eggs and bacon, nod periodically at the conversation going on among the other three people, smile sometimes, and then excuse myself to leave once the coffee is gone. I hope I'm not like this the rest of the trip, because it's rude and I'll never get any good stories this way. There must be something wrong with me because I fleetingly pray that at least a few bad and/or weird things happen to me on this trip. Besides the La-Z-Boy out in the desert. Another seven or eight of those and people will start to wonder if I'm making this stuff up. Which, of course, I would never do.

8:00 a.m.
Just before San Bernadino

I have spotted the first palm trees out the window. I write this down because I live in Pittsburgh. That automatically makes this big news.

8:15 a.m.
San Bernadino

We are currently running about two-and-a-half hours late, meaning our Los Angeles arrival will be closer to 10:45 a.m. than the 8:15 a.m. scheduled time we have just passed. This is perfectly fine with me, even though I'm up, dressed, fed, and packed. I'm about to encounter one of the slight hiccups in my otherwise stellar schedule planning. I booked a moderately priced hotel for my two nights in Los Angeles. And after a bit of searching at the time, finding anything with "Los Angeles" and "moderately priced" was obviously a challenge. But the check-in time for this hotel is three p.m. Their website states that there is an extra $75 fee for early check-in. So much for the "moderately priced" part. I just tried calling the hotel to see how much wiggle room they have in that three p.m. check-in time before they start asking someone to fork over seventy-five bucks. Naturally there seemed to be no good signal out here in the middle of nowhere—wait, we're in San Bernadino.

Having no good explanation for why my call won't go through, I make a mental note to upgrade my phone and plan once I get home. For many years, a prepaid phone plan without any access to data has been fine since I work from home and we have a landline and excellent internet service. It's only at times like this that I grumble. Because there's nothing I can do about it, I am at least glad that we are arriving late, so I will have less time to kill at (another) Union Station. Don't get me wrong: Union Stations are mighty pretty. But the thought of a king-sized bed to myself, a full-sized bathroom with a real, flushing toilet and a huge tub and shower—one that isn't moving and that wasn't just used by a stranger who left his wet washcloth in the stall—is mighty appealing. I'll just have to play it by ear once I get there.

10:10 a.m.
(Another) Union Station, Los Angeles

Figures that I can't even arrive late properly (although I can do just about anything else late without a problem), because we somehow made up a half hour between San Bernadino and Los Angeles. So I still have nearly five hours to kill once I get off the train.

I step off the train, laden with my two traveling companions—the backpack and the messenger bag—and walk all the way from the platform to the heart of the station. The bustling crowd of people around me makes me feel a little wearier than I really am, sucking the energy out of me as they hurry past. This is not just an Amtrak passenger train station, so there are local folks coming and going to various commuter trains also in this station. I keep walking up the main aisle of the station, then right, and step outside into a courtyard that is probably quite lovely when it's not fifty-five degrees, windy, and dreary. It figures I would bring the rainy weather with me from Pittsburgh, to the one place on this trip I would have counted on being sunny, warm, and not rainy.

It doesn't even occur to me that perhaps I would be allowed to use the private Metropolitan Lounge for sleeper car passengers. For the life of me even now, I cannot understand why the idea never crossed my mind, except that maybe my brain had filed that sort of lounge usage for people who are about to get *on* a train and not those who have just gotten *off*. So, I keep hoisting my bags back onto my shoulders, hoping they'll stop getting heavier and more uncooperative, and continue to meander around this busy station looking for a place to just sit and regroup. And now I'm hungry, too.

There are no seats here that aren't either part of a departing passengers general lounge or part of an eatery of some kind, so I give up and choose a place for lunch. The least intimidating for someone in my condition (frazzled, unshowered, casually dressed, and cheap) is a small café near an exit to the courtyard. I sit at one of the cute, but tiny bistro tables and order a simple grilled cheese, fries, and a Coke Zero for about ten bucks plus a tip. I'm not one to complain about simple comfort foods like this, but this one wasn't even all that comforting. I could have made a better grilled cheese sandwich myself if they had let me back into the kitchen. I remind myself that I'm just cranky and a little tired and that at least I didn't have to go back into the kitchen to make it myself. And I won't have to clean up, either. That thought reins in my snark enough for me to continue eating, though

I'm still cranky when it's all over. Plus, they've had a side door open to another small terrace area, and a cold, rainy breeze has been whooshing in. And guess who's sitting closest to that door? This girl. This f-f-f-freezing girl who had hoped to see at least a little bit of Los Angeles sunshine on this trip. I tell myself this will be really funny when I get home and start putting together this part of the trip for the book, but I'm not very convincing when I'm cranky and not getting my way. Who am I kidding? This isn't the least bit funny. I just want a door I can close loudly—with just me on one side of it and absolutely everyone else on the planet on the other side. Is that so much to ask?

I had hoped to sit at this table for a few minutes and check the hotel's website again, and possibly to use some Wi-Fi access to try the Uber app on my not-all-that-smartphone to get me to the hotel later. But (this) Union Station doesn't offer free Wi-Fi, so I knuckle under and spring for $4.99 for a day's worth of Wi-Fi. I use about twenty minutes of it to update Facebook and catch up on a few emails on the laptop, which I am suddenly glad is very small. If I had a 17" laptop like Wayne's, I'd be hurting right about now. And not just because this table is cute, but tiny. His laptop also weighs a ton, and I can already feel my upper body strength getting a serious upgrade having had to carry the stuff I deemed worthy of the backpack and messenger bag. A full-sized laptop would have been a serious mistake.

Despite paying for the Wi-Fi, I still can't get the Uber app on my phone to work. In the dark recesses of my clouded mind, I'm pretty sure there are other options, but since I still have a few hours to kill here so I can avoid that $75 early check-in fee, I don't think much about those.

This place is busy at lunchtime on a Saturday, so I know I can't sit here at this cute, but tiny bistro table for much longer. I give up and get up, glancing around me before hoisting the two bags onto my two shoulders and surveying my very limited options in this station. I don't have any desire whatsoever to head back the way I came, even if they tell me there are lovely galleries or shops that way. The ground under my feet still feels as if it's moving—a phenomenon I've experienced any time I've gotten off a cruise ship—and I want to simply sit somewhere for a bit and gather my wits, what little of them I have left.

I head back outside into the courtyard, even though it's really cold out here and the sky is threatening rain. I sit on a bench in a spot that is probably quite charming on a sunny day in warmer temperatures. There are a few other brave souls out here holding up under the cold, and a few sparse pigeons are prancing around looking for handouts. They don't care what the temperature is. I know you guys are interested in me only because I might have food, but sorry. Slim pickin's today, buddies. If I'd been thinking clearly a half hour ago, I would have saved you some of that unimpressive grilled cheese. You probably would have loved it, and I wouldn't have missed it.

1:30 p.m.

I finally give up on (this) Union Station and even the Uber idea. I've never taken an Uber and this probably isn't a good time to try out a new mode of transportation. Let's just say my husband and I share a motto—"What could go wrong?"—but he says it as an optimist and I usually mean it a little more pessimistically. I figure it's close enough to their three o'clock check-in that I can risk taking a regular ol' cab ride to get to the hotel now. It's only three miles from the station, and I might have walked to the hotel if it weren't rainy and cold, and if I'd brought gear with wheels, and if I weren't me. Oh well. So close.

Once outside on the main sidewalk out front, I see the line of taxis and head in that direction. In the blink of an eye, I'm being whisked around Sunset Boulevard, which is much more winding than I had envisioned. Why do all cab drivers make sure to careen down the street as fast as humanly possible, while looking as if they aren't paying attention to their driving? This guy's fiddling with the GPS mounted on his dashboard, and I swear he hasn't looked at the road in the whole three miles to my hotel. I'm now certain that all cab drivers are hired based on their past NASCAR experience.

I distract myself from his bad driving by looking at the sights outside the cab window. There seem to be a lot of dentist storefronts along Sunset Boulevard. And they all have signs like pawn shops. Also, all places that offer massages call them "friendly massages." I decide I'm too sweet and innocent to think about this any further.

It doesn't matter. We arrive safely, and I'm now twenty bucks lighter ($13.75 for the actual cab fare, and I'm feeling generous so I hand him a twenty and we call it even). Now I know what it will cost me on Monday morning when I head back to the station to catch the Coast Starlight to Emeryville. Pretty sure I'm not going to walk then, either. Pretty sure.

I luck out and the hotel desk clerk here at the Comfort Inn allows me to check in now. I must have looked like someone who would gladly have taken up residence in their lobby for an hour and a half, watching the news on the television and nibbling on snacks, just to avoid an early check-in fee. I snatch the key card, thank the clerk, and whip around the corner to the elevator. I'm only on the second floor but there's no way I'm taking the stairs. Right now I'm all about the comfort. It's a Comfort Inn, after all.

I hold my breath as I open the door to my room, and I'm delighted to see it's a serene, spacious room. The king-sized bed looks glorious. The desk chair is cushy, and the closet has enough hangers for all my shirts. Despite everything having been rolled up and stuffed into a single backpack all week, the blouses are all in good shape and not wrinkled. Of course, I myself feel a bit wrinkled, but no amount of ironing is going to help that.

I claim this space as my own—which I do everywhere—by hanging up all my clothing, setting up the laptop, getting out all the tech gear that needs to be charged or out in the open (phone, tablet, Kindle), and splaying all my mini-toiletries around the bathroom sink and in the shower. I've got a microwave and a mini-fridge in this room, too. I'm pretty sure I've lived in apartments smaller than this, and less well equipped. Life feels good again, and I can feel my equilibrium coming back.

3:00 p.m.

In fact, I feel so good that I'm going to head right down and do this load of laundry I've been accumulating since Monday. I hope they've got a vending machine for laundry detergent and such because I never did solve that laundry pod problem the day I left Pittsburgh.

Grabbing the roll of quarters I've packed, my bag of dirty clothes, and my Kindle, I head downstairs to the main desk (I take the elevator again—I don't feel that good just yet) to ask about the coin-operated laundry they have listed on their website.

"Hi! Where are your laundry facilities?"

"Oh, we don't have any laundry on site."

"But, your website said—"

"Yeah, I know, but we got rid of that. There's a laundromat right across the street, though." The clerk points out the front door behind me to a small strip mall.

"Thanks."

I don't know why I thanked her. I don't feel the least bit thankful about this. But I don't let this wrinkle (so to speak) upset me. I'm brave. I'm fearless. I'm on an adventure. And sure, most people wouldn't call doing one load of laundry in a laundromat in Los Angeles an adventure, but why quibble over matters of semantics? Tomato, tomahto. I *feel* adventurous as I head outside in the cold, dreary, atypical Los Angeles afternoon and walk about twenty-five yards across the street to the laundromat.

It's a compact laundromat, and on a Saturday it's jammed with people. Single guys washing their skinny jeans and bright white T-shirts. Older women who sit at tables in the far corner, chatting. Women with small children who dash around madly, pushing the wheeled carts around like the Daytona 500. I zig-zag around them, trying not to bop any of them on their little heads with my bag-o-laundry. I try not to look out of place here, but it's tough when you're a frumpy, middle-aged goofbag amid a bunch of cool people who probably all know each other. Even the young guy who's working here today is overdressed and over-coiffed.

If he looks this good, then I must stick out like a sore thumb.

I luck out and see a vending machine with single packets of laundry detergent for only $1.25. After the cab ride and the lunch, I feel like I've hit the jackpot. Despite all the people, I find a washing machine easily and it's only three bucks to wash a load. I expected worse. I dump the soap and the clothes into the washer, start it up, and search for an open seat to sit and read while I wait for my clothes to wash. Over my several decades of adulthood I've spent many hours at laundromats. Either I didn't own a washing machine, or when I did, I didn't own a dryer. For many years, when the kids were younger, during my first marriage, I had a low-end Kenmore washer that was a workhorse, but no dryer. I bought a cheap wooden drying rack and learned to do one load of laundry a day so I could drape everything on the rack and around the apartment to dry. Come morning, I'd fold everything up and start all over again with another load. The one-load-a-day theory has not been disproven to this day, and I never feel panic over a "laundry day" filled with load after load.

But I digress. My point is that I sit here in this laundromat, having sat at many laundromats in the past—even across an ocean. Addie and I did laundry while we were in England, in order to save packing space. Plus, it was our own domestic adventure in another country. Of course, we looked like idiots trying to figure out which coins to put in the slots, but eventually we got it right and wore clean, fresh clothing for the second half of the trip.

And I digress again. My point is that I never leave my clothing unattended in a laundromat. Never. I know some people will fill up washers with their personal clothing, start the machines, and then get in their cars and leave.

They just leave! I'm never sure if this represents misplaced and certainly unearned trust or simple naivete (read: stupidity). Either way, it's not how I roll. I sit and guard my clothing at a laundromat. People—dishonest, thieving people—might just skulk into the laundromat (amid all these people) and grab my clothing out of this washing machine (while it's still wet), and make off with it (even though it's mostly from Walmart or a thrift store or the Blair catalog). Then where would I be? I'd be without a lot of my clothes, that's where I'd be. If I were doing this at home because the washer broke, I'd at least have the clothes that were still at the house.

But out west in Los Angeles, when I've packed the bare minimum amount of everything, especially clothing, I cannot afford to let some low-life scum steal my clothes. The thought of having to wear the same clothes I have on now for the next week is enough to keep me glued to this seat in the corner, reading a book on my Kindle but keeping a wary eye on that washing machine in the second row.

All this to say that, well, I find a seat in the corner and continue reading *The Whiskey Rebels* on my Kindle, while keeping a wary eye on that washing machine in the second row. Which I've already just said.

There's a loud sporting event in Spanish on the television right above my head. Somehow I manage to tune it out enough to focus on the reading and the time passes peacefully. By 4:30 the clothes are washed and dried (only fifty cents to dry the whole load! score!), and I fold them and then stuff them back into the Walmart bag I brought them in. I dash back across the street to the hotel and up to my room (still using the elevator—I'm on vacation so why do I think I'm going to take up cardio now?), so I can hang up the clothes right away. They're not a bit wrinkled. I count the laundromat a total success and now I've got clean clothing for the rest of my trip. Unless, of course, I spill something or lose my backpack or... I try not to start making a list of worst-case clothing scenarios. It'll just depress me.

5:00 p.m.
What's for Dinner?

I haven't eaten for about five or six hours now, not even one of my bajillion granola bars. Time to think about dinner. I surveyed the other shops in the strip mall, hoping something there would strike my fancy. But a place called "Donut Farm" doesn't sound like dinner for anybody, least of all a diabetic like me. I grab the Guest Services book out of the desk and find that it suggests using GrubHub.com to order food from nearby restaurants. The laptop is already set up and on, so I head online to see what I can find. I see a place with Chinese food—it's just a chain restaurant called Panda Express, where I've never eaten before. But I figure, how bad can it be if it's Chinese food, one of my personal favorites? Then I remember how often I screw up basic stir fry at home and almost change my mind. Still, the orange chicken and the teriyaki chicken both sound perfect, so I break down and place an online order for both. With the mini-fridge and the microwave, I can save the leftovers for Sunday dinner and not have to go through this again tomorrow.

The good news is that the meal arrives faster than their estimate. The driver calls my cell phone, and I dash downstairs, ready to tip him handsomely for brightening the rest of my evening. He leaves as rapidly as he showed up, and now I've got a bag of hot Chinese food in my hand. I walk around the corner of the lobby to the elevator, glance down, and see that the bag is dripping. Like, seriously leaking. Like, the entire bag must have tipped over in the car on the way here. I wonder about this guy's driving techniques if this bag is leaking this badly. He must be related to the taxi driver I had earlier.

I come back around the corner into the lobby and see some napkins in the corner where they'll set up the continental breakfast in the morning. I mop up the floor where the brown gravy puddle has formed and then hold the stack of napkins under the bag and head upstairs (in the elevator—this is an emergency!).

Once in the room, I hold the leaky bag over the bathroom sink and look around for a possible solution that doesn't involve getting my food any closer to the toilet. On top of the mini-fridge are some glasses and the ice bucket, which all sit on what looks like a common cafeteria tray. With my free hand, I move the ice bucket and glasses onto the microwave and then dump the mushy bag onto the tray. I carefully take the containers out of the wet bag: one for each entree and one with white rice in it. If I use this tray as a sort of plate, I won't have to worry about further leaks.

I will, though, have to worry about how to eat this food. They forgot not only the napkins but also any utensils at all. Not even a plastic spork.

I head back down to the lobby—this time I took the stairs, because, well, gravity—and search the breakfast area for plastic utensils. Nothing. I lucked out with the napkins but nothing else is really out on display, so I meander over to the main desk and sheepishly ask the clerk if he has any plastic forks, explaining (also sheepishly) that the takeout food I'd ordered did not come packed with any utensils. He deftly reaches under the desk and pulls out a bag of plastic forks, handing me one. I thank him profusely, trying not to overthink why they keep an entire bag of plastic forks right under the main desk. I can't think of a single good reason, but it looks clean, so I gratefully accept it and head back upstairs (using the elevator). Crisis averted.

The food is all right, though I'm saddened to find out that you can make Chinese food taste like its own version of McDonald's. I watch some television as I eat, update Facebook (again), and catch up on emails. Then I pack up the rest of the food and put it into the fridge for tomorrow. And I make a mental note to pack a fork the next time I take a trip.

11:00 p.m.

Suddenly, after all the necessary chores of the day are behind me—train arrival, lunch, taxi, hotel, laundry, dinner, laptop work—I find I'm exhausted and want nothing more than to climb into that big, beautiful king-sized bed behind me. My body has decided that it's three hours later than the clocks say. Through Facebook, I've made contact with some local friends who will pick me up in the morning and take me to worship with the Los Angeles Reformed Presbyterian Church, a local congregation belonging to the same denomination I belong to. It'll be earlier than my body likes to wake up, but perhaps I can keep fooling it into thinking we're still on Eastern Time. I set the alarm on my phone, change into my T-shirt and shorts, climb into the big bed with my Kindle, and start nodding off as soon as I swipe it open. It's been a long day. But at least the bed isn't moving. It just feels like it is.

Day Seven

May 7, 2017

8:50 a.m.

Irene and Howard pick me up for church. We have time to kill before the prayer time so they drive us to the famous Forest Lawn Cemetery, all the way up to the peak, where we get out of the car and look down over the valley below. It's an astounding view from up here. The weather's not quite as dreary and cold as yesterday, but it's obvious that it's still not typical Los Angeles weather. I feel as if I should apologize for having brought the weather with me, but of course everyone out here is glad for the rain—any rain. Maybe I should claim credit instead. You're welcome, Los Angeles. You're welcome.

The day is filled with worship and friends and good food and fellowship. The Los Angeles congregation has prayer time, an education class, then worship. After morning worship, everyone sticks around for a fellowship lunch together, followed by worship again at two p.m. I stay with them throughout the day and find that it's good to see familiar faces again in this trip. I soak it up, to carry me through till next Friday when I'm home amid familiar things and people. The Reformed Presbyterian denomination is a funny thing in this way. I've met some of these people before in person, but not all that many. Most I've never met. But somehow we are still a close-knit family and get to know each other with an easy familiarity. I've appreciated that about this crazy group of knuckleheads in the past three decades. And I certainly appreciate it today, when I'm ready to see friendly faces and receive a warm welcome.

Plus, you know, *the food*. This is no Jell-o mold potluck. There's a little bit of everything for lunch, and I find the homemade foods do me good, just as the fellowship does. Take that, Panda Express.

But, eventually all good things come to an end, and by the time Howard and Irene get me back to my hotel after the second worship service, I'm ready for some alone time.

4:00 p.m.

Alone time, in this case, means I won't see anyone I know from now until sometime late on Friday. But that's all right. It's what I signed up for back in January when I booked this trip. And now, only minutes after Irene and Howard drop me off, I hear thunder, and a short downpour breaks out. We've had cool but dry weather most of today, so I'm glad I'm inside now. The rain comes fast and furious, and I watch it from my large window.

Again, you're welcome, Los Angeles. I'm leaving in the morning, so enjoy the rain while you can, folks.

7:00 p.m.

I reheat the leftover Chinese food from last night and start packing up the backpack and the messenger bag. I don't know why I'm surprised when everything fits back in the way I had it before. After all, I practiced packing these things for weeks before I left, worried that I wouldn't be able to fit all the things I'd need. It's still the same stuff it was last weekend when I did my final packing, so it shouldn't surprise me that it all still fits. But it does.

I've got to get up early in order to get down to the train station in time for the Coast Starlight's departure around ten a.m. Okay, that's not ridiculously early for most people, but for me it'll mean getting up around seven a.m. tomorrow morning. The desk clerk told me that all I need to do to get a taxi in the morning is to go down to the desk and ask. But I never trust such things completely, so I'm going to leave enough time for the taxi to lollygag around getting here in the morning.

I turn on the laptop and look through the pictures I've taken so far. In real life, everything looks so much bigger and more majestic than other people's pictures I saw online when I was Googling these places before I left. When I get home, I'll probably get on Facebook and post tiny pictures of my own, with captions like, "Here are some small, non-majestic pictures of huge, amazing places that will give you absolutely no idea of how great this place is. Enjoy!"

Well, seven a.m. is going to come early, so I think I'll turn in earlier than usual just to be sure. Suddenly that midnight departure the night I left doesn't seem so silly. At least I'm wide awake at midnight every night. Not tonight, though. Tonight I will go to bed by eleven. The biggest part of my journey awaits.

Indiegogo Update

May 8, 2017

May 8, 2017

Hi, backers! I'm writing this aboard the Coast Starlight, a leg of the trip running from Los Angeles to Emeryville, California, today. I'll spend about twelve hours on this train, then spend the night in Emeryville since my next train, the California Zephyr, doesn't leave Emeryville till morning.

According to some of the train aficionados on a train forum I've frequented since last year, I've inadvertently booked the wrong cheap motel for the night. One person lovingly referred to it as the Bates Motel. Another bluntly called it a fleabag motel. Both urged me to book something else, anything else. However, I will not be cowed. I am bold and brave and will not give in to fear-mongering tactics.

Plus, I had to prepay up front, so I'd lose that eighty bucks if I canceled.

So, if you're the praying sort, say a quick word that I'm not mugged or beat up on my way to the Bates Fleabag Motel tonight when my train gets in around ten p.m.

Come morning I'll be getting on the Zephyr and heading east… on what many train geeks have said is the most beautiful route to take across the country. Shall we take bets now on whether or not it'll rain?

Day Eight

May 8, 2017

7:30 a.m.
(That Other) Union Station, Los Angeles

Today, at (this) Union Station in Los Angeles, I can sit in the main lobby in the privileged seating for ticketed passengers. Stern warning signs are posted at the entrance to this roped-off section, signs I probably didn't need to heed when I arrived here Saturday morning. In any case, I'm here now and nobody can make me give up this seat. I didn't even need to buy an expensive grilled cheese sandwich to sit here today.

As I sit here munching on another granola bar, happy that I at least chose the kind with chocolate chips in them, I overhear a mother speaking to her small child behind me:

"Are you going to let her stand on your face like that?"

I decide not to turn around to see exactly what's going on. It's a lot more fun to imagine it.

There's a piano in the lobby with a small sign inviting people to sit and play. On Saturday, it soothed the soul of this savage (cranky) beast to hear lots of people playing. Some were quite good. Needless to say, none of them were me. I haven't taken piano lessons since the eighth grade, and my recent attempts to remember how to play now that we have a piano in our house have been abysmal. Worse than abysmal. I sometimes practice when nobody's home (because I love my husband too much), and even I can barely stand to hear me play. But the people here on Saturday who wandered over to the piano and tickled the ivories were good. Truly good. And no "Chopsticks."

Apparently today, though, nobody feels like playing the piano this early in the morning because the area is closed off. I'm guessing that commuters don't reserve time in their Monday morning schedules to stop and play the piano on their way to work. It's too crazy-busy with people in here today. I'm happy to be sitting off to the side watching them all come and go, knowing I don't have to move until it's time to board the train. I'm here. I'm safe. I'm in the right place. And I won't miss my train. Logistics and schedules make me tired.

A woman dressed like Mother Teresa keeps walking around the station. She's not carrying anything. She's just meandering around. I see her pass again and again, and I wonder what she's up to. She doesn't look frazzled. She's probably not commuting to work. She doesn't seem lost or confused. I find this ridiculously fascinating. There's a story here that I don't know, that I'll never know (because there's no way I'm getting out of this chair to go ask her, only to find out she's just looking for a restroom).

The people who populate busy train stations (aside from many of the commuters) are a more diverse group than I've seen at airports. In fact, anyone who looks like they'd fit in better at an airport is probably just a commuter and looks almost out of place here near the Amtrak people. It's a unique group I travel with, to be sure.

8:00 a.m.

It's hard to believe that only a week ago I was at home packing for this trip. At home, a week goes by and many of the days seem largely the same. I like my little routine at home—it's easy, it's familiar, and it involves a lot of coffee and computers and no alarm clocks. This past week has turned all that on its head, and I've learned how to adapt to ever-changing situations. The rest of the trip will require more adapting because I won't have any more time off the train with familiar faces to buoy me up. Just me, some trains, and people I've never met and will likely never see again.

Thinking of the trip so far, I realize that the Amish never made it all the way west with me. Or, if they're here, they're hiding really well. Instead I get to watch a hipster couple, both in skinny jeans and matching new white sneakers, walking in step together down the main aisle of this lobby. It's alternately humorous and scary. I'll let my thoughts venture elsewhere while I think it's humorous.

I like to notice what people are carrying as they dash to and fro here. I think I can tell the commuters from the Amtrak passengers. This early in the morning, most of the people dashing around are probably commuters. I do notice that large plastic bags are the new Samsonite. They're everywhere. I can't imagine being saddled with plastic bags with flimsy handles. I can barely handle just these two bags with proper straps and handles everywhere.

8:20 a.m.

I get a seriously pleasant surprise. I'm sitting here, minding my own business, and I hear an announcement over the P.A. system saying something about Train 14. I double-check my e-ticket and see that the train I'm waiting for is Train 14. The train isn't scheduled to leave till 10:15 a.m., but since I hear only part of the announcement, I worry that something has changed and decide to leave my sacred chair and head to the Information Desk just around the corner to ask about my train.

The man at the counter takes a look at my e-ticket and sees that I've booked a roomette on the Coast Starlight this morning. He informs me that I therefore have access to the private Metropolitan Lounge for ticketed sleeper car passengers. I had completely forgotten that there is such a thing. So, even as I sat here wondering if booking the roomette for a long day trip was overkill, the question was answered for me. No, it wasn't overkill. I get to use the private lounge! I take a last glance at the cordoned-off section for coach passengers that I have just left, and I feel a momentary pang of sympathy before thinking, "Goodbye, suckers!"

8:45 a.m.
Metropolitan Lounge, (Another) Union Station, Los Angeles

So now it's comfy chairs and free coffee and fruit and the news on a big-ass TV, our very own clean restrooms with large stalls, and a table of my own to spread out and do some writing on the Alphasmart. I put my backpack off in a corner with everyone else's and settle in. Sure, I was happy enough with the general lounge area for the commoners downstairs, but I'm much happier up here. I've paid a lot of money for this trip, so a little pampering by Amtrak staff here and there certainly won't go unappreciated. I get a little gushy with the woman who checks me in, and she seems pleased that it takes so little to make me happy. Low maintenance. Always low maintenance.

I'll get to sit in calm, peaceful quiet for the next hour-plus till we board. Nice. I'm still a little nervous about how tonight will go—with the Bates Fleabag Motel awaiting me—but I'll jump off that bridge when I come to it.

Now I won't miss the train, either. The Metropolitan Lounge makes sure everyone leaves for the platform in plenty of time. In fact, we get priority boarding ahead of the lowly, common, unwashed masses downstairs. Yeah, I'm liking this upgraded treatment. Good thing it hasn't gone to my head.

Of course, the main trade-off in being upstairs here is that I give up the people-watching downstairs in the main lobby of the station. I decide that I took enough notes for all that and would rather be up here with all the amenities.

I admit I've had a few moments of homesickness in the past week. Not major, but moments where I've thought that it will be nice to be home on Friday. Evidently I'm more a creature of routine than I care to admit. And I think that's precisely what's at the center of the homesickness: just wanting a little more routine than I'm getting on this trip. My gosh, I'm getting old. I can almost feel it. (Hash mark.)

9:00 a.m.

Okay, here's the down side of this lounge. The TV is way too loud and *Let's Make a Deal* just came on.

9:15 a.m.

Wow, someone just won a set of accessories, mostly shoes and purses, worth $7,000. My car isn't worth that much money. Shoes and purses? Low maintenance, lowwww maintenance. It's becoming a sort of mantra by now. I watch for a few more minutes and start to wonder if Wayne Brady ever feels as if he's sold out.

I daydream about what I'll do on board the train today on my way to Emeryville, California. I'll probably write an update for Indiegogo, which I'll upload once I'm at the motel. I'll take more notes on things that happened over the weekend. And I'll get lots of views of the Pacific Ocean, which I have never seen.

The coffee is kicking in now, and my stress levels are lowering again. Of course, I'll feel even better tomorrow morning at this time, when I'm sitting at the Emeryville Amtrak station, with the Bates Fleabag Motel experience behind me and with nothing but trains ahead of me till I get to Pittsburgh.

As we wind down our time here in the Metropolitan Lounge, I see an ad on the television for puppy loans. Yes, that's exactly what it sounds like. Out here in California, you can apparently take out a loan to buy a purebred puppy. If it were me, I'd just sell the $7,000 in shoes and purses to buy that puppy.

9:45 a.m.

I'm on the Coast Starlight now, in Car 1430, Roomette #2, upstairs in a longer hallway of roomettes. I'll have a slightly different view from up here. I got a Red Cap golf cart escort from the lounge to the door of Car 1430 on a beautiful sunny morning. It figures that the weather goes gorgeous on the morning I'm leaving. This doesn't surprise me. The ride was well worth what I tipped him. There's nothing fun about having to walk the entire length of the train just to get to your car.

We leave in about a half hour. I think the coach passengers haven't boarded yet, but I'm already settled into my room and have my laptop open here on the tiny fold-out table. I'm unsure if I'll be facing forward or not once the train starts moving, so I might be switching to the seat facing me if the train isn't going in the direction I first assumed.

When I first come into the roomette, both pillows are on the seat across from me, plus two coat hangers. I take the empty seat. It happens to also be on the right when standing in the doorway, just as I sat in the roomette on the Southwest Chief. Creature of habit. That's me.

I like this longer hallway of roomettes. It feels like a tiny college dormitory of trains. I hear the voice of a smaller child somewhere down the hall, but of course I'm not going to allow that to bother or influence me in any way. Unless the kid starts shrieking. Then it'll bother me.

10:00 a.m.

We seem to be settling in to something like a pre-departure routine. A Metrolink commuter train or two has left on other tracks.

Melody, our supervisor today, just came past and introduced herself. I have no idea what a supervisor does on an Amtrak train, but she had on a blazer and was carrying a Starbucks coffee. So obviously she's pretty important.

I'm ready for my day trip.

10:15 a.m.

We're departing on time from Los Angeles. And, although I had a 50/50 shot at picking the right seat, I chose unwisely. For the first few minutes I don't realize it and think perhaps I'll stay facing backwards. Then I change my mind and figure it'll be more natural to see what's coming up (since you can see a little bit ahead of you when facing forward), at least in terms of taking pictures out the windows. I'm happy to see that these windows are clean, inside and out, so I expect the pictures to be decent today.

I'll see how this train compares to the Southwest Chief as far as the smell emanating from the chemical toilets. That might be an odor that lingers in the senses even after one gets off the train.

Perhaps it's just my own familiarity with how things work on a train now, but today seems calmer and more pleasant than on the Southwest Chief. Perhaps it's because I made it through the morning in great form like a real grown-up: getting up on time, making it to the station by cab with no hassles and no traffic), realizing I could sit in the Metropolitan Lounge, taking the Red Cap cart all the way to the train, and ending with a more pleasant aroma in this train. We'll see whether it's because the train has been freshly cleaned, whether it'll remain this pleasant till tonight. And of course, once I get on the California Zephyr tomorrow morning, I'll really see how things hold up through traveling from Tuesday morning into late Thursday afternoon.

My Sleeping Car Attendant for the day is "T," and she's in the roomette just across the hall from me. I could tell that was the roomette reserved for the SCA when I first got on board, but I hadn't realized that "T" was my SCA till she went in like she owned the place and sat down. Now that I've seen how hard these folks work, I'm glad she gets some time to sit. Then again, I'm an introvert and would not last long in a job like this. I think I'd manage if forced, but I'd have to end every work day with a good cleansing cry all by myself.

10:53 a.m.

We've passed Van Nuys. I'm treated to the view of the backyards of houses along the route. Some of these are a little nicer than ones I saw on the Southwest Chief, but most have brown—*TUNNEL!*—lawns. Oops, sorry about that. I didn't see it coming, but we just zipped through another pitch-black tunnel. It's a weird sensation when you're not in your car where you can see it coming.

There are a few yards that seem to have perfect green lawns, till I realize that it's artificial turf and not actually grass. It looks just too perfect to be real grass, especially here in California with its water shortage/drought issues. I'm not a big fan of yard work, so I tuck this idea away for our unruly half acre at home. I wonder how long it would take Wayne to notice the grass isn't real.

1:00 p.m.
Lunch in the Dining Car

I am seated once again with just one other person, a man traveling home to San Francisco from Arkansas. Surely nothing is quite as awkward as continuing to have meals seated alone with one man. I need to get better at math and to glance into the dining car to see where I will end up before committing to being seated next. Surely even an English major can learn to count to four. I thought an introvert's worst nightmare would be eating a meal with three other people I don't know. It turns out the nightmare is being seated with one other person I don't know. I'm already doing the math on how many more times I might be subjected to this situation this week. Short answer? Too many. So... much... math...

I choose the Southwest Entree Salad for lunch, which includes chicken and guacamole and edamame on romaine lettuce. I even took a picture, like a good geek nerd wannabe.

Mid-Afternoon
San Luis Obispo

There is a young couple standing outside the train here at our smoke break stop. They have matching ball caps. I'd say it's adorable, but I wonder whether they're doing it so they can find each other in a crowd. You know, the way whole families wear matching T-shirts to Disney World. He's wearing black Crocs, so I think I'm right. The couples I've seen on this trip have all been rather darling. Well, except the hipsters.

We are told over the P.A. system that there will be no dinner reservations. I think they say because there are few enough people on the train that we just won't need reservations. Again, fine with me. The fewer people, the better. Of course, that might mean I get stuck with just one meal companion again if they decide to let us spread out in the dining car. I secretly hope that I choose the perfect time for dinner so that I get a table to myself. I also secretly wish that I didn't already know this is never going to happen.

Late Afternoon
Still San Luis Obispo

We are finally leaving San Luis Obispo after a delay of nearly two hours. This will get us into Emeryville quite late, which doesn't make me happy. I'm already unsettled about the thought of getting into a town after dark and having to find my way to my Bates Fleabag Motel. So now I'm praying that I get to the motel in safety. Also, the later we get in, the less sleep I'll get before having to get up and get back to the Emeryville station in the morning. These mornings are going to kill me. Night owls deserve better schedules than this.

5:46 p.m.

TUNNEL!

Stray Thought #1: Now we're moving slowly around all the curves because we have to, despite being a few hours behind schedule. It's clear to me that, if you travel by train, you do it partly for the experience. There is just no way it can be about the efficiency of getting where you're going.

Stray Thought #2: Going around these curves, with so many hills and mountains blocking my view, I don't know what's coming up around the next corner. It's a marvelous feeling if it's your first time seeing all these sights. A surprise every time you look out the window.

6:00 p.m.
Dinner in the Dining Car

I sit with a lovely couple from the Bay Area who are gracious enough to answer questions I have about local foliage I'm seeing out my windows. It never occurred to me that the trees and bushes would all look different out here—well, aside from the palm trees. Those I expected. I may not know much about botany (which is clear to my dinner companions), but I'm not a complete idiot. Most of the time.

I have the chicken fettuccine again, mostly because I don't want to try to knife through a steak with strangers watching me.

We comment a lot on the scenery and they answer a lot more questions about the trees. They look pleased that they get to look really smart without much effort.

It would be a lot like them visiting Pittsburgh and asking, "Hey, what are these little pockets of dough with potatoes, cheese, and onion inside?"

"Oh, those? They're pierogies. Try one."

"We've never seen anything like this at home!"

"Just think of them as Eastern European raviolis."

"Oh, you are so wise!"

"Thanks. I try."

At one point we pass a huge (huge!) parking lot that isn't attached to a store or anything. It's just a parking lot out in the middle of nowhere. The jokes about free parking flow like wine. We laugh and giggle as if we've actually been drinking wine. We probably should be. I find that most of the fascinating man-made sights outside my windows have been out in the middle of nowhere. I'm pretty sure that doesn't really mean anything significant, but like most of my small, petty observations, I'm mentioning it anyway.

Dinner ends on a happy note and I feel I have made some friends at this meal. I go back to my roomette content and happy.

If only that contentment could have lasted.

This Chapter Isn't Funny

May 8, 2017

We end up nearly two hours behind schedule. This worries me. I already didn't like the idea of getting in at ten p.m. and then having to get a cab to a potentially seedy area of town. I try not to let it worry me... but it does.

We arrive in Emeryville, California, at nearly midnight. The station is deserted. Only a few of us get off the train at this stop, and I seem to be the only one heading all the way to the station, down the long platform. I go into the station, only to be told by an attendant that they are locking up the station for the night. I ask if I can hit the ATM first—I don't want to end up in a cab without enough money. I probably have enough money, but one can never be too sure.

I get $100 in twenties out of the ATM. Amazingly, there is already a $20 bill sitting in the tray before my money is dispensed. Someone has left it here. And since no one else is around, there is no way to find out its owner. So I take it and consider it a good sign.

I am wrong. It's not.

I walk out the other side of the station where a sign says "Taxis." Another woman from the train is here, and immediately her Lyft driver shows up. I try to wave to the attendant I spoke with inside, who is now getting in her car. She had told me from inside, when I asked about getting a cab, "Sure, go out this other door." Which I just did. And now the other woman is gone in her Lyft car, and the attendant is also gone. One last woman also steps outside the station and I ask if she's waiting for a cab—I think perhaps we can share—but she is local and simply awaiting her husband, who arrives within minutes, and now she too is gone.

By now I am sweaty and upset and scared. I'm beginning to hate the word "adventure" and realize I have been a fool to want one.

I'm about to be locked out of this building, with no data on my prepaid-minutes phone, which means I can't get on the internet to look up the number of a cab company. Needless to say, there are no available Wi-Fi hotspots showing up, either.

One last attendant comes outside. When I ask about a cab, he asks if I have a smartphone. I explain the no-data thing, and he (rightly) looks at me as if I live sometime in the last century. I kinda do. He kindly suggests that I take the high catwalk from the station across to the Hyatt House hotel, which apparently isn't far. By this point I'm willing to pay for a close, SAFE hotel and no cab ride at all.

The attendant lets me walk through the station to the other side, near the catwalk, and then locks up behind me. I find the sound a little bit jarring, and now I truly am alone.

I find the industrial freight elevator to take me up to the catwalk, adjust my backpack and messenger bags on my shoulders, and step out onto the catwalk. Up here, above the ground, looking out in the dark over the station on one side and the hotel parking lot on the other, I begin praying like I haven't prayed in a long time. Many years ago, when I felt this alone because I truly was, the prayers were personal, intimate, and intense. This experience is no different. All I ask for is safety. Protection. I can handle lack of sleep. I can even handle not finding a place to stay tonight, though the thought of curling up here in this concrete and steel catwalk isn't a pleasant one. The Fleabag Bates Motel is starting to seem not so terrible to me now.

For a few brief moments, when I'm alone up here in the night and have all my possessions on me but nowhere to go, I feel homeless. If you ever think that being rootless or homeless might have some strange element of adventure, think again. It is terrifying to be without any moorings whatsoever, with absolutely no one knowing where you are. It's not cute or funny like Steve Martin carrying a chair and a thermos in *The Jerk*. I do not recommend it. At all.

At the end of the catwalk, I take the elevator down (because I have now decided that I will take every elevator I see from now on—stairways be damned) and am in the parking lot of the Hyatt House. The lot didn't look this big when I was up on the catwalk, and it seems to take forever for me to reach the hotel. And, of course, the door is around the other side. The backpack and messenger bag keep gaining weight with every step. But at least now I can see the light at the end of this personal tunnel.

I step into the Hyatt House and nearly collapse at the front desk. I explain my dilemma, and I'm told they have no rooms left. None. On a Monday night in the off season. This does not please me, but I can't say that I'm overly surprised. I'm still currently safe, though, so my prayers are at least being heard. But I'm only human, so I continue to worry. And to pray.

I hold myself together, but it's obvious to them I'm pretty upset. One of the two men manning the desk, José, is exceptionally kind and calls the nearby Hilton Garden Inn and finds that they have a room available. I feel my heart stop and then start again. José then calls a cab for me. I take a seat in the lobby across from the front desk, sigh, and wait.

A few minutes later, they tell me it looks like my cab is waiting outside. Sure enough, the phone rings, and José says, "Your cab is outside. They just called." The relief keeps flooding through me. I thank the desk clerks profusely—to the point of embarrassment, I'm sure. I must look like a pathetic, mixed-up, rootless woman who showed up in this lovely hotel in the middle of the night, out of breath and obviously out of options.

I head outside, open the back door of the Lyft driver's car that's waiting there, and say hello. She turns to me, smartphone in her hand, and says, "Are you Eric?"

I joke that, at this point, I'm willing to let her call me anything she wants, but it's clear that someone else is meant to have this ride. But there are no other cabs or Ubers or Lyfts in sight, so I'm again befuddled by what's happening.

Back inside, I tell José that the car out front is not for me, which perplexes him. After another phone call, he finds out that the cab driver mistakenly went to the Hyatt *Place* hotel nearby instead of this Hyatt *House* hotel. This is apparently not an isolated incident, and I can see why. So I go stand outside, to be out in the breeze where I can breathe more easily, and await the right cab driver.

For ten bucks I get a very short cab ride to the Hilton Garden Inn, which is less than a half mile away. I no longer care. After all, I had a lucky day, right? I found twenty bucks in an ATM.

I'm treated well at the front desk of the Hilton Garden Inn, for which I'm grateful. But because I'm a very-last-minute walk-in, I pay $239 plus taxes and fees so I can sleep for a few hours in a small, though comfortable room. It'll average about $40 an hour to stay here. The room's so small that I have to move the desk chair out of the way to get around it because it bumps into the bed. Good thing I don't really need to get around to that other side of the bed.

Perhaps the best part of this deal for me tonight is that this hotel has a free shuttle to the train station, so I don't have to get a cab in the morning or walk.

So... let's recap.

The **good news** is that I gained $20 in the bank machine.

The **bad news** is that I lost $239+ on the second hotel, plus the $84 I prepaid for the Fleabag Bates Motel.

The **good news** is that I save some money on cab fares, both to this hotel (because it was close) and to the train station tomorrow because of the shuttle.

The **bad news** is that I won't save nearly enough money to make up for the price of this small hotel room, even if it is lovely.

The **good news** is that I'm safe and I have a place to sleep tonight.

The **bad news** is that it's now nearly two a.m. and I'll be getting about four hours of sleep. I'm really cranky when I don't get enough sleep.

The **good** news, though, is that I am indeed safe, which was my original prayer. That's very good news.

I dump all my stuff onto the bed, pull the money and credit cards out of my jeans pocket where I've stashed them, collapse to my knees on the floor, and start sobbing. I can't remember the last time I've been this scared, or ironically, felt this protected. It's over. The worst is over, and now I can focus on the rest of the trip, including the glorious fifty-four-hour California Zephyr trip that starts in the morning.

Despite my earlier calculations, this is definitely not a hotel that charges by the hour (*wink wink, nudge nudge*), but somehow I still feel like I got screwed today.

Okay, sure, tonight's escapades cost me a bunch more money than I had intended, but I realize it isn't about money. I was almost stranded all alone outside a deserted train station after midnight in a town I don't know, and now here I am safe in a lovely (small) hotel room where I'll be able to sleep in peace. In the morning I can shower and get ready for the big part of my train adventure. And a free shuttle will take me back to the station.

Thank you, Lord. I am safe.

Day Nine

May 9, 2017

7:30 a.m.
Hilton Garden Inn, Emeryville, California

The Hilton Garden Inn's shuttle to the Amtrak station will make my morning calmer and more pleasant than I can say. I got only four-and-a-half hours of sleep last night, but so far I'm feeling okay. I used the cute little Keurig in the hotel room to whip up a quick coffee, ate a few more granola bars, and headed down to the lobby to await the shuttle. I sit on a comfy chair in the sunlight and take a few deep, calming breaths. Still, I can feel I'm already tired. It'll likely be an early night for me. As I continue munching my makeshift breakfast, I make a mental note to never buy granola bars ever again.

7:45 a.m.
Amtrak Station, Emeryville, California

Everything looks so different this morning. So different from the way it looked last night when it was deserted and I was desperate. Now it's bustling with activity, with sunshine pouring through the windows. I might not have been as frightened last night if I had seen this version of the station first.

I have time to kill before we board the Zephyr, so I turn to my usual hobby of people-watching. One of the two sets of sliding doors out to the platform doesn't work, and I sit here watching dozens of people walk all the way up to the defective doors, expecting to trigger them open when they stand in front of them. When the doors don't open, most folks figure out they aren't working and then move to the set of sliding doors at the other end of the room. But it takes some people longer than others to figure this out, which, I confess, amuses me as they stand in front of the doors waiting for them to open. It's like my own personal episode of *Candid Camera*.

One guy is walking a small dog (which they are transporting in a sort of baby stroller with netting over it) and physically shoves the doors open, takes the dog outside, then comes back in the same doors and shoves them closed again. I'm not sure whether to be impressed or to think he's an idiot. Probably a little of both.

A station agent calls all us California Zephyr riders to the platform outside just before the train arrives. I'm in the sleeper car at the very front of the train, meaning I'll have a long walk to the diner and observation car once we're on board. That's okay. If I'm going to live on this train for more than two days, a little exercise certainly won't kill me.

Unless I trip and fall while the train's moving and bang my head on the wall or fall down the staircase. Then maybe it'll kill me.

I hoist the backpack over my right shoulder and the messenger bag over my left. Might as well get started. We have to walk quite a way down the platform. The folks behind me are joking about it, and it does seem a bit ridiculous. Nothing to be done about it, though. I murmur that we are apparently walking to Chicago.

9:15 a.m.
On Board the California Zephyr

My e-ticket says I'm in Car 640, Roomette 17, but this is a "different consist," according to Dave, my Sleeping Car Attendant, so it's actually Room 3. Whatever. More math. Upstairs, next to his Room 1. I like the upstairs better, for some reason. Maybe because it's a bit farther away from the conglomeration of three restrooms and the shower. I don't mind the stairs once I'm not carrying all my gear.

Tonight will be the first time I've traveled overnight with people occupying the roomette across the hall from me. On Friday I had no one across the aisle. Yesterday was only a long day trip, with "T" in her roomette only now and then throughout the day. From Emeryville to Chicago, I will have a married couple, approximately my age, across from me. This is their first time in a sleeper, which I find quaint. Apparently I already consider myself an expert on train travel. If I could, I'd smack myself right now for thinking such idiotic thoughts.

Anyway, I can't wait to hear what they think of the roomette come tomorrow morning, especially whichever one of them gets to sleep on the top bunk. I'm finding I have absolutely no curiosity about trying that, even if it would mean a funny chapter in the book. Then again, after last night's scary hotel fiasco, redefining the word "adventure" to mean nothing more than sleeping in the top bunk in a roomette on an Amtrak train sounds about my speed.

I fiddle around on the laptop, toying with some ideas for Facebook posts. Perhaps:

"I just had an adventure. I don't recommend it."

Or maybe this:

"Last night's adventure at Emeryville, stranded after midnight in a deserted station they were locking up for the night, with no way to call a cab... Adventures are highly overrated."

Probably this:

"This will be funny someday... in 2047."

This is the longest stretch of "train" on my journey, and of course I end up with a folding tray table that's off kilter. It slants downhill and I can't seem to find a good spot to keep the little laptop flat. And yes, I'm the person who gets the shopping cart with one wobbly wheel. This is a lot like that.

This train doesn't have Wi-Fi, either, which might be a good thing in terms of book writing, but which pisses me off just the same. Boy, I'm really cranky when I get half a night's sleep.

Despite the Wi-Fi thing, I suddenly feel so calm and relaxed. The things that had been worrying me for the past week are behind me, and although things turned out to be more expensive, at least I was safe. Now, if only they could get funnier.

12:30 p.m.

I think I'll try having lunch in my room today. I'm feeling a little wiped out after yesterday and last night, and I think one meal where I'm not "peopling" would be good for me. Plus, I'd like to try the Angus Burger, and it seems like a potential mess to eat in front of strangers. I'd rather avoid that embarrassment by eating it alone in private.

Even though meals are included in my ticket price, I tip David five bucks because he has to put in the order and then bring it to me. As soon as he shows up with my meal, I know it's totally worth it. The Angus Burger is a bit messy, though I think I could have managed it in the dining car, depending on my lunch companions. The burger was quite good, and the kettle chips and deli pickle are a nice complement. Add a Diet Pepsi (with caffeine I'm going to need for the rest of the day), and this is one seriously great lunch. I might do this for lunch tomorrow too, now that I've found the introvert's loophole in the whole dining car experience. I'm pretty sure I've had enough experiences for the rest of the day.

After lunch I grab my Neo, Kindle, and camera and head for the observation car, which is three sleeper cars and the dining car past my roomette. It's seriously crowded in here, and despite warnings not to put belongings on the seats to reserve them, a bunch of people are doing just that. I sit at a table at the far end of the car with one other man. I'm facing backwards and have some trouble getting good pictures. Granted, part of this is that I suck at photography, no matter how good a camera you give me.

While I sit at this table in the observation car, taking pictures of snow on the mountains (in May!), I get a sudden flash of happiness and contentment. After last night's hotel fiasco, this surprises me and I have to force myself not to cry. Part of it might be the severe lack of sleep, but some of it is just that I periodically remember that I AM DOING IT. I'm on my big bucket list trip, the number-one item on my bucket list. It won't be a "someday I'll do this" thing anymore. I'm really here, right now, on trains, going across the entire country. I'm seeing—up close—beautiful vistas and changing scenery. I'm seeing the whole country. I never thought I'd do it.

But, if that trip to England in 2008 with Addie taught me anything, it's that there's no time like the present. If you can make something happen sooner rather than later, do it. I can only hope to continue to implement this thinking in other areas of life, including even the small things such as remodeling projects, spending more time with family and friends, finishing all those books that are partway done. Why have I been waiting to do any of these things?

I'm in the observation car for about ten minutes before there is a call over the P.A. system from the dining car attendant that at least one person from each sleeper car room needs to go back to the room. He'll be coming around to take dinner reservations soon. So, I pack everything back up and off I go, right back to the ol' roomette. Well, at least I got some exercise for the day.

3:00 p.m.
Somewhere near Truckee, California

We're going through an unusually long tunnel and it's starting to affect the smell of the air inside the train. I know there was a discussion about this on the Amtrak Unlimited forums. Something about the tunnel being so long that the fuel fumes build up while the train's in the tunnel. I bet it smells just wonderful outside the train.

I look from my roomette window up at the snow-covered hillsides beside me and get choked up again. Man, am I behind on sleep. I think I've figured out why this is happening, and it's not just the lack of sleep. I think it's that I'm seeing so much of God's creative hand all around me. So many different types of flora, fauna, rock formations, everything. How can you see all this variety, all this majesty, and not believe in a God who made it?

Oh, a side note: the snow-covered "hillsides" of the last paragraph are the Sierra Nevada Mountains. "Hillsides"? I am the master of the understatement.

4:30 p.m.
Just Past Reno, Nevada

We're told over the P.A. system that we're now at a spot where we might (theoretically) see wild mustangs. This excites me greatly and I drop what I'm doing and start staring out the window, camera in hand. Soon, I see one: a dead one on the side of the road that's all ribs and a little bit of skin/hair stretched over half his body, his head mostly intact. Mostly. I decide not to take a picture.

5:00 p.m.
Dinner in the Dining Car

I had dinner with a woman named Eileen and a man whose name I have forgotten. (I'll ask him if I see him again on this trip.) Both are from California. She is thinking of moving to Utah. She was an English teacher, went to NYU. I give them my business cards, and we have a lovely conversation about writing and property values and education. It makes me think that perhaps the mealtimes can be redeemed after all. Having had lunch and dinner with just that one man on the Southwest Chief, I'd begun to think they would all be awkward events, especially for an introvert. But if they're like this, it'll all be good. The dining car has been bustling and full, as is the train itself, so I suspect I won't be sitting with just one other person anymore, especially an awkward one. I've got my fingers crossed that my hunch is correct.

I can't believe it, but I've chosen the chicken fettuccine yet again. That's three dinners, all the same. I was sitting with two people who don't eat red meat so that turned out to be the fortuitously wise choice. Steak tomorrow? We'll see. I had the lemon tart for dessert, which was pretty good. And the pièce de résistance? Not having to cook it or do the dishes. Score.

6:30 p.m.

I'm back in the roomette relaxing and typing up more notes... and staring out the window again. I figure I might as well stare and gawk while it's light out. The view out your window changes so fast that if you look down for too long, you miss an important change in the scenery. Once it's dark there's really nothing to look at, so then I'll read. If I'm even still awake then. I think tonight will be an early night for me. I have no idea how I'll want to handle breakfast, but we'll see how it goes. There are a lot of people on this train so I might have to wait for a shower. And I'm hoping that hot water doesn't become an issue, with so many of us on the train.

7:45 p.m.

I saw whatever type of jackrabbit or hare would frequent the Nevada desert area go racing away from us across some sand and a lot of dry brush. Would be fun to see a coyote and a road runner out here. Or even just an anvil.

7:49 p.m.

Just saw another small herd of cows go racing away from the train. I'm surprised at how fast they can move. The calves are way ahead of their mothers. Kinda like taking my kids to the grocery store.

We're supposed to set our phones/clocks/watches ahead one hour overnight. We'll wake up back in Mountain Time. Wasn't I just in Mountain Time a few days ago? I only need to know so that I'm not late for a meal.

8:06 p.m.

It's creeping up on sundown. I'm watching the mountains off in the distance, along with trucks on the far highway. And there's a glorious full moon overhead. I could sit and look at this for a long time. I think I will. I'll probably nod off and bang my head against the window.

8:14 p.m.

And just like that, the train has turned and banked and the moon is no longer in my view, the trucks are on the other side, and the sunset is mostly gone. Within minutes it'll be too dark to see anything. Our section of the hallway all seems to want their beds turned down around 10:30 tonight so I went with that too, so poor David doesn't have to scurry back here for one person. So I'll read in between now and then, take my meds (because I'm old now and meds are a thing—another hash mark), and try desperately to stay awake. Boy, that doesn't sound like me. This time of night is typically when I'm just starting to wind up for hours of work. Anyway, now I have to find my gray shorts and hope I didn't leave them in the hotel.

FOUND. Right on top in the front pocket of the backpack. Clearly I am a blind idiot. Clearly I need sleep.

8:25 p.m.

It's not quite pitch black outside the window, but it's getting there. I can see where there's a body of water because it shines and reflects off the full moon when it's on my side of the train. I find this simple thing amazing to look at.

In the dark, with just the moon visible, if the train banks and curves at a decent speed, but I can't see exactly how or when it's curving, it looks as if the moon is racing across the sky and back. I'm delighted that simple things like this thrill me. It's making the trip so much more than mere transportation, which was mostly the point in the first place.

Day Ten

May 10, 2017

7:30 a.m.

I slept well last night. I sat up reading till around eleven p.m. (Pacific Daylight Time, though I'd already turned my phone's clock back to Mountain Time), and then went to sleep and didn't stir till five a.m. (Mountain Time—are you keeping up with this?), when the whistle blew and we made a stop somewhere in Utah. I went back to sleep for a few more hours.

Why do I keep getting up so early? Oh yeah, I keep going to bed at a decent hour. I gotta do something about this when I get home. Honestly, there's something just not right about it. And today I prove it to myself. I head to the bathroom just down our hall and lock myself in, double-checking the lock, as usual. At some point in the, umm, proceedings, I accidentally hit the call button here inside the bathroom.

Until now, I didn't realize these tiny bathrooms had a call button. I can see why they would. There could be all sorts of emergencies happening in here at any given moment: running out of toilet paper, the teeny water faucet going haywire and spraying water all over, the train lurching and a passenger bumping his head on the wall. The buttons are necessary. Fair enough.

But honestly, they should give the rest of us ample and clear warning about these call buttons. The room is small enough that it's entirely possible to accidentally bump the call button while going about one's business, as I have just proved. I'm thankful no audible buzzer or alarm went off—that would be just my luck, wouldn't it?—so I don't think too much about it, figuring I just brushed up against it and no harm done... until an attendant starts knocking on the door from the outside.

"Is everything all right?"

I have a split second to decide whether to respond, and if so, how. My early-morning brain is completely out of practice, but it occurs to me that saying nothing will mean the attendant might fear the worst (that I've fallen down the toilet and onto the tracks below) and unlock the door from the outside to check on me. So, I'll have to say something. And soon.

I go with the generic and non-revealing reply:

"Everything's fine! Sorry!"

I try to disguise my voice a bit, so that, if it's David out there, he doesn't know later that it was me in here right now.

"Okay!"

I hear footsteps—or is that just the train?—and wait a

few minutes before unlocking the door and peeking out into the hallway. I can only see to the right until I step out of the bathroom completely and close the door, so I start praying that David isn't standing just down the hallway to the left. As deftly as I can while on a moving train in the morning before I've had coffee, I step out, close the door, and tiptoe back toward my roomette. Nobody's around and I make it back without being seen. Crisis averted.

Later, I realize that I can't be the only person to have done this, and all attendants probably answer false alarms more than actual emergencies in these bathrooms. At least I hope so, for their sakes.

8:00 a.m.
Breakfast in the Dining Car

There isn't a line for the shower this morning, so I get right in, shower without touching the walls or any other linens left behind, get dressed, and make it back to my roomette in an efficient manner. Breakfast is calling, so I close the door and head down to the dining car. I'm getting really good at tapping the sliding pocket doors between cars just right so that they zap open easily and don't slow me down. The first day on the train, I had a hard time finding the sweet spot on those huge handle-buttons that activate the automatic doors between cars. Like everything else on a train, it just takes a little getting used to.

I'm seated at a table first, alone, since I came in without other people around me. Eventually we add John and his adult son, Matt, to the table. They're from Ohio, and the country is so big and this trip is so expansive that I feel I have just met next-door neighbors. After I mention I'm on this train to write a book about my bucket list trip, we talk about Beverly Lewis fiction, and Gettysburg, and the flatness of Ohio and Indiana compared to the majestic views we have out our window as we eat. As someone who routinely eats her breakfast alone at her desk most mornings, I'm shocked to find how pleasant sharing a morning meal with other people can be. I don't get this experience much at home because I feed Wayne breakfast at about 6:50 a.m. and he dashes out the door to work around 6:55 a.m. Essentially, he inhales food and then leaves. I go back to bed and eat several hours later.

Before John and Matt arrive, though, the attendant takes my order after asking if I want coffee. I'm surprised this isn't a rhetorical question at breakfast, so I assure her that yes, I need coffee, and then I order the bacon and eggs, as usual.

"Would you like some cereal? French toast?"

"No, thank you. I can't have any carbs at breakfast."

"Maybe some potatoes or grits?"

"Thank you, no. Really, no carbs for me. I can't handle them in the morning."

"How about a croissant then?"

Clearly she is not familiar with the term "carbohydrate."

I smile and thank her again and say that the simple, boring scrambled eggs and bacon will be great.

When she brings the eggs and bacon, she points out the basket on the table, noting the breakfast syrup, jellies, and jams.

Thanks, they'll go great with that no-carb breakfast I told you about earlier. Yes, thank you.

The dining car experience is good again this morning, though I keep thinking it's still weird to walk into the dining car, only to have someone say to you, "Sit here. With these people you've never met. And eat food. Which you will probably spill all over your shirt. Because we're making you eat on a moving train. Oh, and here are some sharp utensils and a cup of overfilled hot coffee. Good luck! You're on your own!" The klutzy introvert's worst nightmare. Generally speaking, the last time I felt this much apprehension was giving an oral report in sixth grade. But at least then I wasn't going to drip syrup on my shirt or give myself second-degree burns with a cup of coffee.

10:00 a.m.

We were in Utah overnight and this morning but have apparently moved into Colorado. I have been trying not to be disappointed that there aren't big black lines on the ground delineating the states' boundaries. You know, like on a map.

After breakfast, I hear a bunch of folks talking about various animals they're seeing. There have been sightings of mountain lions, buffalo, some sort of deer (I wonder if they had big white butts), a fox, and others. I think we're seeing more animals than they saw on that first Jurassic Park tour. I may spend more time staring out the window for a while today, unless something more important comes up. Which, you know, it won't.

It's rainy today (of course it is), but still gorgeous in its own way. The clouds hang low and you can see the mist and water in the air. Somehow, Pittsburgh in the rain doesn't look nearly this lovely.

The P.A. system crackles to life: we're in the Grand Valley, Western Slopes, and we'll be stopping at Grand Junction, Colorado, for about ten minutes.

10:42 a.m.
Grand Junction, Colorado

I see a tumbling tumbleweed. A real one, just like in all the movies and TV shows. Granted, this would have been far more exciting if it hadn't been on a sidewalk next to a train track. Still, I'm stoked.

As we leave Grand Junction station, we get the typical Welcome Aboard rules and list of do's and don'ts. Those always include the one about not smoking anywhere on the train. We are cheerfully reminded that, if we're caught smoking on this train, we'll be taken off the train by local law enforcement. I have two stray thoughts about this:

- Do they wait till the next stop, or do they just cavalierly toss people off the back of the caboose like in the movies?
- This is the kind of threat that would never work on an airplane.

More random thoughts (which all belie my accumulating lack of sleep):

- As of this year, I've been online for thirty years.
- Putting eye drops in your eyes while you're on a moving train can be hazardous to your health.
- At home, I have a lovely dining room. Seriously, lovely. But somehow, it's going to feel as if it's missing something when I get home and sit there eating a meal, disappointed that I look out the window and the view never changes, that I won't see the Rockies going by, or a herd of antelope, or even a dead wild mustang. Then again, perhaps not seeing the dead mustang is all right.

- I think it's dangerous for me to have this much time to myself, with my own undivided attention.

11:36 a.m.

I just saw a wild turkey.

Out the window, of course. The bird, not the bourbon.

There's a guy driving a pickup truck with an open trailer attached zooming down the highway parallel to the train tracks. Two tumbleweeds are stuck in the grates of the trailer, and it looks as if he's carting them somewhere on purpose. Is there some sort of Tumbleweeds R Us outlet around here?

12:33 p.m.

We're in Glenwood Springs Canyon. I see a large, lone doe of some variety of deer. It reminds me of our Pennsylvania white-tailed deer, and I wish I could have gotten a picture of her. I could have taunted my dad with pictures of big hunting game since he never sees any when he's actually hunting.

1:00 p.m.
Lunch

I chicken out and opt for another Angus Burger in my roomette. I tell myself I have a good excuse, though. The dining car keeps filling up and they are now taking names for a waiting list. I am feeling a bit "peopled out" anyway and enjoy the privacy of this yummy lunch in my roomette. Plus, you know, the not-cooking and not-cleaning-up thing.

3:15 p.m.

After eating, the sightseeing begins in earnest. We pass through Glenwood Springs Canyon, where I take way too many photos that will probably look the same once I get home, and there's still some rain lingering. After this we hit Gore Canyon, with 1,500-foot dropoffs from the cliffs into the Colorado River below, with its Category 5 rapids. I can all too vividly picture this entire train just tipping over and down into the gorge, never to be heard from again. Maybe I don't need to have my face pressed so close to the glass. I'm scaring myself.

Right now we're back on prairie-like ground with a lot of cattle and a spotting of houses, surrounded by majestic rounded peaks on all sides. We crawled through Gore Canyon, and let me tell you, some of the tracks are perched a little too precariously on the edge for me. It makes for some amazing views, though, as long as you don't think too much about exactly where you are.

5:00 p.m.

Now we're in the foothills above Denver, Colorado, in the Rockies. I'm actually riding along the Rocky Mountains. Sometimes I have to remind myself that I'm really here, that I'm not watching this on television or on a YouTube video anymore. It's almost unreal. Almost.

According to another announcement over the P.A. system, we've just stopped because of a possible rock slide on the tracks ahead of us. Right now we don't know any more than this. From what I've read online, the conductors are the ones who have to go out and check on things like this and move debris out of the way. Boy, there's a fun job for you. If there's snow still out in places like this in May, I can only imagine what fun it would be to have to do this in February. I remind myself never to apply for a train conductor's job, which won't be all that hard for me to remember.

Animal Update for this afternoon: I'm seeing lots of pairs of geese on the Colorado River. I even saw an entire goose family with at least a half dozen goslings. I also see large white birds, slightly larger than the geese, with long yellow-orange beaks. They're also floating on the water as the geese are. Are they swans? Ducks seem to be omnipresent. Add on a few eagles or hawks circling above and you've got quite the traveling aviary to look at from this tiny roomette.

I made my dinner reservation for 6:30 this evening. I hope to get through dinner quickly tonight. I feel not only sleepy but more introverted than usual. (Some days I suspect that's not even possible, but today it feels true enough.) I just wish to be left alone for a little while, so now my introverted brain keeps checking the time and is starting to dread the arrival of dinnertime. (That's saying something, since I tend to never dread dinnertime. Or any mealtime, for that matter.) Of course, if it's a full table again tonight, I'll have the option of quietly nodding and listening to the conversation rather than participating.

6:30 p.m.
Dinner in the Dining Car
Denver, Colorado

Dinner is lovely... again. I don't know why I knee-jerk all the way to fear at the thought of sharing a table with several other people. I wouldn't have guessed that I'd prefer a full train where they fill up every table with four people to an emptier train where I sit with just one other person. Tonight I sit with a couple from the United Kingdom who flew from London to San Francisco and are now traveling by train back to New York, where they'll get on the Queen Mary to head back home. Planes, trains, automobiles, and cruise ships! That is quite a trip. I may have to add a few things to my bucket list now that I'm going to cross this one off the top.

Our other table companion is a man from New York who was a teacher and did volunteer work in radio, reading for the blind. He has one of those voices you could listen to for hours, so I see why he would have been great at his volunteer work. Despite my introversion, the storyteller in me loves the variety of people who travel by train. People-watching in an airport or train station is great fun, sure. But people talking and people sharing is a lot better. Even I can agree with that.

For dinner, I finally have the steak, rare. It is wonderful. I'm glad I finally tried it. We eat our dinner looking out on the rail yard here in Denver since it's a long stop and all trains have to back into the station, for some reason.

Now we're on our way again and are traveling past the typical industrial plant views so often seen near railroad tracks. Most of the many tracks are for freight trains, which also explains why we sometimes have to stop to allow the freight trains the right of way.

8:30 p.m.

This time tomorrow I'll be on my final train, the Capitol Limited again, heading from Chicago back to Pittsburgh.

The Zephyr will arrive in Chicago a little before three p.m. and then I kill some time in (that) Union Station till the Capitol Limited leaves a little before seven p.m. I think I have all the logistics worked out for my arrival in Pittsburgh at the tail end of the trip, which will come very early in the morning. It's around forty miles from the Pittsburgh (sometimes Union, sometimes Penn) Station to my house in New Brighton. Calculating possible cab fares made me weak in the knees, so I've decided to use Wi-Fi in Chicago to look up fares and schedules for the Beaver County Transit Authority buses heading from downtown Pittsburgh up to the very street where I live. It's gotta work out, even if I have to take a short cab ride to get to the closest bus stop from the train station. I try not to wish (again) that I'd brought gear with wheels. I'll fret over that decision later, but not today.

And now, I think I'm done writing for the day. It's getting dark and it's rainy (which is an utter surprise, right?), so I can't stare out the window anymore. Well, I can, but it'd be pointless. It's time to get out the Kindle and read before getting into bed. Of course, getting into bed on a train typically involves the Sleeping Car Attendant (in a strictly platonic way), so once he comes by later to do his presto-change-o magic trick with my room, I'll curl up with the Kindle and enjoy my last night on the California Zephyr.

Day Eleven

May 11, 2017

7:45 a.m.

I'm up, showered, and at breakfast. This was my last shower on the trains because tonight's Capitol Limited excursion ends tomorrow morning around five a.m. I plan to go home and sleep, and I'll worry about personal hygiene a little later.

Scrambled eggs, bacon, coffee. Breakfast of champions. It might seem like I'm in a rut, but at home I have just the scrambled eggs and coffee. Every day. It's a diabetic thing. I wasn't just hassling that dining car attendant when I said that I can't handle carbs at breakfast. I really can't. In addition, I just shouldn't. I like eggs, and I'd rather "save" some carbs for later meals, when my blood sugar can better handle them. I'm as far from being a morning person as a person can get without being a vampire (well, except for the drinking blood thing), so any feeling of routine and habit means I can be half asleep in the morning while I'm making breakfast. I go on autopilot, make a couple of scrambled eggs, turn on the coffeemaker that I prepped earlier, and take the concoctions upstairs to my desk, as I do every morning.

On the train, of course, that entire routine has been thrown off. The times are earlier. The getting showered and dressed is earlier—and, in fact, now comes before the coffee and eggs, which I have found deeply disturbing. Eggs and coffee are meant to be enjoyed in a nightshirt, at a big desk with a computer sporting a dual-monitor setup, the coffee staying piping hot on a mug warmer, the eggs being wolfed down immediately. Then, around noon, I take the dirty dishes downstairs, refill the coffee mug, and head back upstairs to finally shower and dress. You know, in case other human beings insist that I appear out in public. Like, going out the front door to check the mailbox.

So, it's unnatural to wake, grab toiletries, and head down a semi-public moving hallway to a tiny semi-public moving shower, where I'll shower and try not to die an ignominious death by misadventure. Then I'll try not to soak my clean clothing while I'm trying to dress in the semi-public moving shower. Only then will I head back to my roomette, dump the toiletries back into the messenger bag, grab my phone, and walk all the way to the dining car, trying to deftly smack open the automatic pocket doors between cars and to walk down the passenger hallways in other sleeper cars along the way, hoping I don't accidentally tip into someone's open-doored room when the train lurches. Because the train always lurches when I'm walking down a hallway.

Let's face it: nearly everyone looks like a drunken sailor walking through the cars of a train while it's moving.

1:30 p.m.

I wimp out and ask for lunch in my roomette one last time. The Angus Burger it is, one last time. I spend the extra time packing and repacking my backpack and messenger bag. We're due to get in to Chicago just before three p.m. and I want to be able to get off the train and into the Metropolitan Lounge in (that) Union Station as efficiently as possible. The scenes out the window now are a lot less majestic, but I've been on this journey long enough that I don't mind seeing more urban, slightly more familiar surroundings. The foliage looks familiar. The landscapes look more like what I'm used to. I miss seeing the mountains, but I'll remember riding through them and being so close for so many miles and hours. And, as much as I'm ready to be home, I also can't wait for another train adventure in my future. Maybe next time I'll go somewhere with a friend.

I look around at the roomette, up at the tiny second bunk tucked away above me. It'll have to be a really good friend.

3:45 p.m.
(The First) Union Station, Chicago

I'm here in (this) Union Station in Chicago. I've got a few hours until the Capitol Limited takes me on the last leg of my excursion, home to Pittsburgh. I took the sluggard's route and let the Red Cap golf cart whisk me from the train platform all the way to the door of the Metropolitan Lounge. It's far better to bring enough money to tip Red Caps when there's no good reason to traipse the long distance from the train to the lounge. Maybe next time I'll choose a normal suitcase or carry-on with wheels. No matter what I choose, I know there'll be a next time.

The Metropolitan Lounge is bustling, people coming in and others leaving as their trains are called for boarding. I'm near the front at a table, across from the counter that holds coffee machines and dispensers full of nuts, trail mix, and other snacks. I've got my coffee and a little bowl of snacks here as I check online to find the schedules for the port authority bus to take me from the Pittsburgh station to my house tomorrow morning. Looks like I'll have my choice of buses leaving at regular intervals down near the station since it's a weekday during rush hour.

Of course, I can't get a good sense of just what "near the station" means in this case. I again mentally smack myself for not getting a backpack with wheels because the thought of lugging both of these bags (which seem to increase in dead weight every time I have to lug them somewhere) for any appreciable distance seems daunting. If it turns out to be too far for my out-of-shape body and psyche (remember: old, hash mark), so early in the morning after what will likely be a crappy night's sleep, I might take a cab to the bus stop. Sure, that'd feel like defeat in a way, but I'll just have to adjust my expectations and ask myself what I need to do in order to get to the tail end of this trip. The train adventure will be over by then, so I'm sure I'll quickly revert to my unheroic, self-interested, cranky self and opt for the easiest, smoothest way to get from the last train to my home.

I've still got a little time to kill, so I'll do some people-watching. Being so close to the hub of activity, here near the food and the front of the lounge, I get to see everyone who comes in or leaves. A woman walks up to the snack dispensers wearing a gaudy floral dress made out of yards and yard of material. She's wearing a big, floofy wig that looks as if it's perched on top of her head like a curly bird's nest. It's the same gray hue as sticks and twigs, lending credence to my bird's nest theory. It's not just me who finds her interesting. Others around her are doing subtle double-takes in her direction. I hide a snarky smile in case she turns around and sees me. I decide to admire her for dressing the way she wants, even if it's a bit flamboyant. I dress the way I want, too, but it's almost always T-shirts and jeans and a pair of Chuck Taylors. Very blend-in-able, which is what an introvert likes. If I'm going to be stuck in a crowd of strangers like this, I'm going to want to blend in as much as humanly possible. Almost every piece of clothing I packed for this trip screams, "Move along! Nothing to see here!"

5:30 p.m.

Still hanging out here inside the Metropolitan Lounge for ticketed sleeper car passengers. An Amish family, including two young children not much older than toddlers, is hovering around the snack dispensers. Picture typical Amish clothing—black pants or pinafores, solid-colored shirts, caps or straw hats. You can see it in your mind's eye even now. This is how the parents look. Now picture more of this typical Amish clothing, only in teeny tiny proportions for someone who's no more than three feet tall. Right down to the cap on the little girl and the straw hat on the boy. They're so adorable and cheerful and well behaved that I just want to leap out of my seat and go hug them both.

But I suspect the authorities would find something illegal in such behavior, so I just jot down notes about it instead.

Their heavily bearded father helps his two children use the drink dispenser and hands each one a plastic cup of cranberry juice. He himself carries two other cups—one of which is presumably for his wife, who has gone on ahead of them to find some seating—and at least one of the cups has Pepsi in it. I find this strangely amusing. And, I'm tickled to see that the Amish have rejoined me as my odyssey winds down. It's not quite as interesting as the two dozen who were obviously stalking me ten nights ago as I left, but this sweet family is a nice addition to my final evening.

6:00 p.m.

We'll be boarding soon. I've shut down the laptop and packed up the messenger bag again so I'll be ready as soon as they call us for boarding. I have a few minutes to simply watch people as they pass by. I see so many women carrying what appear to be extravagant, expensive purses, often very large ones. I don't know if it's my stubborn low-maintenance personality, or the fact that I spent a lot of my early adult years being desperately poor, but I don't really get the idea of a lavishly expensive purse. Aren't purses merely bags to carry your valuables? Does it make any sense to use a purse that costs ten times what all the stuff inside it is worth? How have the purses become more valuable than the valuables? Clearly there is something I'm missing about the whole phenomenon.

There it is! An announcement over the P.A. system here. Time to board, so off I go. My final train awaits.

Indiegogo Update
May 11, 2017

May 11, 2017

Well, hello again, backers! Why did I bring all these *business cards*? I mean, seriously. Surely I should have realized that an introvert will not start shoving business cards into everybody's hands as we pass each other in the narrow corridors. Maybe I'll leave a few in the restrooms, kinda like Chick tracts.

I'm giving some of them out at meals if someone asks why I'm on the train—which is the standard, compulsory question among dinner companions at every meal. (It's a slight variation on the "Where are you headed?" question you hear on an airplane. This one is, "Why are you on a *train*?")

But honestly, why did I think I'd need 150 of these things on this trip?

Note to self: When you get home, fill out that application for Overthinkers Anonymous.

Day Twelve

May 11–12, 2017

7:00 p.m.
On Board the Capitol Limited

Here I am, nestled snugly in my last roomette: Car 3009, Room 19. We're not even past the urban Chicago area and I just saw a coyote. Or maybe it's a wolf. Obviously I can't tell the difference, although I can tell a gray squirrel from a fox squirrel at a hundred paces. The creature is walking along the tracks less than a mile from the Horseshoe Casino, in this urban area. Now I've seen just about everything. And I think I've said that before on this trip.

We're getting a quick dinner here on board, so I opt for a private audience with one last rare steak. It's as yummy as the one I had last night on the California Zephyr, and it's my last meal on the train during this pilgrimage. I thoroughly enjoy it, and I watch the scenery outside my window as much as I can, even if it's not quite as spectacular as it was on the Zephyr. I'm trying to soak in as much train-ness as possible while I still can. After all, the number-one item on my bucket list these past few decades of adulthood is rapidly fading away and will soon be crossed off forever. I'm torn between the weariness that wants its own bed and familiar surroundings and the sadness that comes at the end of a much-anticipated experience.

So, I finish my steak, sit back, and watch out the window as the world goes by, as my world gets ever closer. No more hurried notes to type. No more pictures to take. Just time to pass, time to feel the train's movement and try to remember it later once I am home in my stationary house. I'm a lot more pensive than I expected to be right now. But perhaps that's fitting. I'll never be on my first train trip again. The next time it will all be familiar and comfortable. I'll know my options. I won't be afraid of anything. Just as I'm not afraid now. From now on it's mostly about the logistics of getting home.

10:30 p.m.

I'm turning in for the night. The Sleeping Car Attendant knows when each of us is scheduled to get off the train, so he'll awaken us in time for our scheduled five a.m. stop in Pittsburgh. Do these guys ever get to sleep through the night? I doubt it. I set an alarm on my phone for four a.m. to be sure I'm wide awake and ready to grab my bags and hop off. One last night to doze off to the comforting rocking of the rails.

5:30 a.m.
Penn Station, Pittsburgh

I lumber off the Capitol Limited, my backpack and messenger bag each slung over a shoulder, and make my way all the way along the platform to the steps leading down to the station where this all began. The sun isn't up yet and it feels as if I am skulking away in the middle of the night. I was awake before the Sleeping Car Attendant was scheduled to awaken me. I dressed, put on my shoes, and opened the roomette door so he'd know I was already up. And then the train stopped and I knew I was back in Pittsburgh.

And now I'm back in this small, yet functional station. I grab a seat in the same spot where I started out, near the door, with my gear in the adjoining seat. I get out the notes I took on bus stops and prices and stare at it for a while. I'm too tired and it's not sinking in. All I keep thinking is that I should probably wait till it's light out and then find a way to get a cab to the nearest bus stop, where the first bus will arrive a little after seven a.m. I have plenty of cash for a short cab ride, and the thought of walking to the bus suddenly seems like more than I'm up for. My brain is still fuzzy, and I can feel adrenaline still buzzing in my system. It'll be like this till I walk off the bus near my house.

6:45 a.m.

Even though everyone whose stop was Pittsburgh has already left the station, there are still plenty of people here. These are folks who are leaving Pittsburgh for other destinations or who are here from the Capitol Limited but who are transferring to other trains later today. I finally decide to go scout out a cab. The first Beaver County buses will be downtown now to take people northwest of the city. Time to close out the great train trek.

I stand and hoist the bags onto my shoulders again, walk outside, and look around. No cars. No cabs. It hadn't occurred to me that, because this is a small station, the passengers getting off here and staying here aren't all that numerous—not like a city such as Chicago or Los Angeles. There isn't really a cab stand here, which, deep down, I already knew if I'd been paying attention the night I got here. But my mind was on other things then and I had my own personal taxi driver in Fara.

There's an information desk inside, so back in I go. I ask the clerk if there will be more taxis outside. No, not routinely. Not now. They were probably here right when we arrived, but I've let that opportunity slip by.

I could ask the clerk to dig up the number of a cab company, but I wonder if perhaps I can walk to the bus stop after all. Even if it takes me a while, even if I miss this bus and have to wait for the next one, maybe this is the thing to do.

Stepping outside, I adjust my bags higher on my shoulders and head off down Liberty Avenue to the intersection where the Beaver County bus will arrive. I'm surprised to find that it's only about four blocks from the station, and despite the bags slipping off my shoulders every few minutes, I get to the bus stop with about ten minutes to spare. I'm the only one here, but this doesn't surprise me. At this time of morning on a weekday, most folks will be heading into town, not out of it, especially from Beaver County forty miles away.

7:15 a.m.

The Beaver County Transit Authority bus stops in front of me. I've got my $3.25 in quarters clutched tightly in my hand and step on board, both bags dangerously close to sliding down off my shoulders again. The coins drop into the coin box one by one, and I find a seat near the front. Bus aisles are even narrower than train corridors so I don't want to navigate any more of this aisle than I have to when it's time to get off the bus.

I settle in among the commuters, who all seem to know the bus driver by name, and sigh. I started out this journey thinking I would need to spend nearly $100 on a cab ride home from the station because I knew the Pittsburgh PAT buses didn't travel far enough into Beaver County. I'd completely forgotten that a Beaver County bus makes the trip all the way down to Pittsburgh and back a few times throughout the day.

So, I've offset that expensive last-minute hotel back in Emeryville by about half by taking this bus for a couple of bucks in quarters. And it's one of the nice, long-distance buses, so I'm comfortable. And suddenly sleepy. I can feel the adrenaline seeping out of my system. It's been a long trip.

8:30 a.m.

The bus stops two blocks from my house after I pull the cord to alert the driver that I'd like to get off. It drives off and before I know it I'm walking through the front gate, up the steps, and I'm in the house. I drop my gear and head into the kitchen. The kitchen island's covered by eleven days' worth of mail. There aren't really any dirty dishes in the sink. Wayne's been feeding himself with fast food or casino buffets in my absence. There will be laundry, though, and not just mine. But all of that can wait. Wayne's at work for the day, and the bed is calling me. Nothing in my bags needs immediate attention, so I leave them on the floor in the foyer and climb the stairs to the bedroom. To the bed. To long, untroubled, unmoving sleep.

As I drift off, my mind forever crosses the number-one item off my bucket list. And I think, very briefly before sleep takes over, that I'll have to add other adventures to the list before it's too late. But of course, it's never really too late for an adventure, is it?

All aboarrrrrrd!

Debriefing: Extra Stuff

Indiegogo Updates
After the Trip

May 20, 2017

Real Life Encroaches

I've been back from my cross-country bucket-list train trip for about a week now. Hard to tell exactly, though, because my brain hasn't fully adjusted to having a routine again.

That's probably because I had to make three long car trips up east of the city this first week back:

- one to pick up the **guinea pigs** (and apparently guinea pigs do not appreciate being stuffed into a small plastic box and carted fifty miles in a car while "Weird Al" Yankovic music is blaring over the car speakers);

- one to join my daughters on a **house-hunting spree** (which included one house where we were counting the bullet holes in the windows and matching up the trajectories of similar holes found in the dining room wall—just like an episode of *CSI,* yay!);
- and one to attend a standing-room-only **memorial service** for the wife of my first Reformed Presbyterian pastor.

Talk about a week of ups and downs! My heart is full.

At home I've been trying to:

- catch up on **freelance work**;
- sort through 1,500 pictures and 20,000 words of notes from the trip;
- do **laundry** (apparently people like to wear clean underwear around here—how rude);
- go **grocery shopping** (apparently these same people appreciate eating several times per day—every day);
- stare at the waving fields of wheat in our backyard. Well, it's just **uncut grass**, because the lawn mower Wayne ordered in early April still needs to be picked up in Calcutta—Ohio, not India (though, judging from how long it's taking him to go get it, I'm beginning to wonder if it's not in India).

No matter what, though, I'm still organizing those trip notes and am now buckling down to turn all this raw data into *Train of Thought* this summer. Those of you who backed me here on Indiegogo (and thank you for that!) will be glad to know that I'll be contacting you soon about mailing addresses for hard copies of the book and email addresses for the Kindle editions.

Other than all that... I think I need a nap. One in a real bed that doesn't convert back into a cute little seat on a train once morning hits. Having said that, I do miss someone else cooking all my meals and sometimes serving them to me in my private little room. Those rare steaks were pretty good! Maybe I'll grill a few ribeyes this weekend... if I can find the grill amid the wheat fields.

June 6, 2017

Anybody know what month it is? What day of the week? Whether it's day or night?

I'm feeling a bit rootless since getting home from my trip about three weeks ago. I'm still organizing my notes for the book, and I've got the main gist of how to write the book. I like where it's headed... except for one teeny chapter that still hasn't become funny yet.

It involves one scary late night in California. I might need to percolate on this particular entry until I find the humor in it. My life motto is usually "Find the Funny" because it's always there... somewhere. This one's been a little tough, though.

Of course, I could simply say, "Eh, screw it!" and call that chapter, "This Chapter Isn't Funny."

But that feels like cheating. So, I'll polish the other chapters around this one until I can find the funny. It's there, somewhere. It's just hiding.

Things, and Other Things

Things I'm Glad I Brought

- **The granola bars.** They have saved my blood sugar more than once when I ended up at a station or hotel at a bad time of day or went too long between meals on the train (usually my own fault). Since they're the chewy kind, they're holding up well, not crumbling into tiny dry pieces like regular granola bars. But I bought too many so I'm still eating them three months later.

- **The good camera.** It took pretty great pictures even through a dirty roomette window. I tend to take blurry pictures anyway, but this thing is doing great with the focus and battery life. (I have spare batteries but will likely not even need them. Here's to clear pictures!)

- **The Kindle.** Once it's dark on the train, the observation car becomes a moot point. Although last night the full moon was beautiful reflecting off the water, a lot of the time it was appearing to my neighbors across the hall and not me. Plus, how long can you stare at the moon before you get an urge to start howling? The Kindle to the rescue! No Wi-Fi, and I've been taking notes all day anyway. After dark on a train is the perfect time to sit and read.

Things I Didn't Use

- **Most of the granola bars.** I could have pulverized them into liquid form and fed them to myself intravenously 24/7 and still not have run out of them.

- **The earplugs,** though I wondered on the Zephyr if I might need them since something out in the hallway was banging around loudly. I wasn't able to pinpoint what it was, but it didn't happen that last night so I slept fine and didn't use the earplugs.

- **The iPod.** I also brought my generic, one-inch-square, clip-on MP3 player that has a thousand songs on it. It's got great battery life so when I wanted to muffle out that banging noise I just put the ear buds in. Didn't need the bigger iPod after all.

- **The travel mug.** I simply used Amtrak's paper coffee cups at meals, and since I actually made it to breakfast, I had my morning coffee there in the dining car. After about Day Three I hated lugging that travel mug around.

- **The voice recorder.** Between the tiny laptop, the paper notebook, and the Neo, I had every opportunity to type or write out my thoughts or other things I want to remember for later. The voice recorder is small, so it wasn't a big space hog to pack, but I hadn't anticipated how little I might need it in such close quarters. Plus, I prefer typing out my thoughts to speaking, so if I have access to two small devices for typing and one for recording my voice, I'll choose the typers every time.

- **The lovely sandals.** Everyone must wear shoes on the train, except inside our private rooms, and when I wasn't fully shod in the Chuck Taylors, then I used the cheap flip-flops for things like getting up in the middle of the night or heading to the shower. And if it wasn't too cool in the train during the day, I kept the flip-flops on then, too. They were more comfortable than the sandals (which are fairly new and not broken in very well yet) and served the purpose well. Lesson learned.

- **The second pair of sneakers.** Doesn't mean it wasn't a good idea to have them, just in case, but I wore them only to church on Sunday, and I could have worn the sandals. (You know, the sandals I shouldn't have brought. See above.) I'm so low maintenance that I needed only two pairs of shoes. This is why the *Let's Make a Deal* prize of shoes and purses confused me.

- **All these PENS.** I kept using the same cheap pink clicker pen I started out with (and mostly because a clicker pen fits so well inside the spirals of the *Train of Thought* notebook I brought from Shutterfly). At least pens aren't heavy.

- **All these BUSINESS CARDS.** I bought 250 *Train of Thought* business cards specifically for this trip. Now that I'm home, I have no idea what I'm going to do with the other 240 of them.

- **The first aid kit and the sewing kit and the Tide stick.** Those were unnecessary. Fine with me. Needing any of those three things would have been bad in its own way. I'm mostly surprised about the Tide stick. Somehow I didn't spill salsa all over me at a meal on a moving train.

- **Three copies of all my paperwork.** I used one printout of the QR scanner code and itinerary of my trip. The multiple emergency copies stayed tucked away in my messenger bag. I was sure I'd need a fresh printout every few days. Paranoid? Not me.

- **So many pairs of earrings.** Honestly, I wore a pair while I was at Sarah's house, I wore a pair for church on Sunday in Los Angeles, and I wore a pair the day I got on the Zephyr. The rest of the time I didn't bother. The only time I was forced to interact with other people was during mealtimes in the dining car, and everybody was either staring out the window at the passing scenery or trying not to spill their drinks on their shirts, like me.

- **The money belt.** When I felt vulnerable (see Day Eight), I simply stuffed all my credit cards and cash and I.D. and the paperwork for the e-ticket in a front jeans pocket (which is nice and deep) and had everything on my person. The money belt was a moot point because I spent so much time on the train and not really sight-seeing off the train. A money belt is useful in crowds, not trains.

Lesson learned: Believe it or not, even a single backpack and messenger bag for a twelve-day trip can be considered overpacking.

But don't overthink it. Pack up and **GO!**

About the Author

In the early 1980s, Linda pursued a writing degree from Carnegie Mellon University in Pittsburgh, Pa. She pursued it, but it kept getting away.

She has since worked behind the scenes in publishing as a proofreader, typesetter, and copy editor. She's worked with publishers, big and small, and with individual authors, big and small. (The big ones really ought to get a little more exercise.) She's also an eighth grade composition coach for WriteAtHome.com.

Linda is currently on the board of the St. Davids Christian Writers' Association and also the board of education and publication of the Reformed Presbyterian Church of North America. She also serves as author liaison for the Beaver County BookFest in Pennsylvania. It's a shame she doesn't get paid for any of these things.

Her favorite writing challenge since 2004 has been the yearly contest known as National Novel Writing Month: writing 50,000 words of a single new fiction project during the month of November. She loves the pressure of a ridiculous, forced deadline. To make matters worse, she uses a typewriter. She's won NaNoWriMo every year since 2004.

Linda also enjoys comedy, computer gadgets, office supplies, reading, movies, adventure games, crocheting—and her office guinea pigs, who keep her company while she's working. Clearly she's an adrenaline junkie.

She currently lives in western Pennsylvania with her husband, Wayne Parker. They share six children between them, all of them now grown and living their own sometimes humorous stories.

Visit Linda online:
www.lindaau.com

Follow Linda on Twitter:
@LindaMAu

Stalk Linda on Facebook:
www.facebook.com/AuthorLindaMAu/

Look at Linda's stuff on Instagram:
@austruck1

54107006R00110

Made in the USA
Middletown, DE
02 December 2017